BEADING
ON A
LOOM

A BEADWORK HOW-TO BOOK

BEADING ON A LOOM

Don Pierce

INTERWEAVE PRESS

Graphs for planning loomwork are included on pages 107–110. Please feel free to photocopy and use them for your projects.

Editor, Judith Durant
Cover design, Bren Frisch
Production, Dean Howes, Andy Webber
Illustrations, Gayle Ford, Jason Reid, Dean Howes

Cover: *Purple and Friends* by Don Pierce. Photograph by Joe Coca.

Beadwork Magazine
Interweave Press, Inc.
201 East Fourth Street
Loveland, Colorado 80537-5655
USA

Printed in the United States by Vision Graphics

Library of Congress Cataloging-in-Publication Data

CIP applied for.

First printing: IWP—10M:399:VG

It was a dark and stormy night. I was hanging in a shadowy doorway on a narrow street in Santa Fe. The snow was drifting down like white ghosts. I was deliberating about my next meal. Crab cakes at the Coyote Café or lamb chops at Café Pasqual's. Life is full of hard decisions.

Suddenly I heard heels clicking on the sidewalk. Out of the swirling snow a vision appeared. She was dressed all in white from her white lizard cowboy boots to her white Stetson. A real dish.

"Hey old timer," she said, her voice like warm honey on a hot biscuit, "why are you standing out here in the snow?" "Just waiting for you doll," I said. "Well," she said, "what do you say we get together and do a book?"

"What the heck," I said. "Why not?"

ACKNOWLEDGEMENTS

Placing the Blame

Just in case this book bombs, I think it's important to spread the blame a bit. There is no reason for me to catch all the heat.

I blame old and new friends for their encouragement. A lot of blame has to go to my wife Janet for having beads in the house in the first place and for putting up with my brief periods of temperamental behavior during the book's writing. Virginia Blakelock comes in for a share of blame because it was her work that turned my feet down the pathway of the loom. Martin Kilmer, Jim Thornton, and Joe Coca get the blame for photography. Several people including Jeanne Boardman Bard, Benson Lanford, and Jack Heriard furnished me with invaluable material help. Then there are the artists whose work appears in the gallery section. They get a big share of the blame—and my gratitude for allowing me to share their work with you.

The most blame goes to my editor Judith Durant who took all the disorganized, fragmented, poorly-thought-out-stuff I sent her and pushed, prodded, and shaped it into a book. She is a lady of great patience. She and all the fine staff at Interweave have been great.

Now, on the other hand, if this book is a great success, then of course I will be happy to take *all* the credit.

Table of Contents

SOME HISTORICAL BACKGROUND

This purse and the one shown at right are fine examples of the European bead weaving that was done from the seventeenth through the early twentieth centuries. The French or Austrian purses are of silk thread and cut metal beads. This purse, probably from the early nineteenth century, measures 7" × 10" plus fringe. From the collection of Jeanne Boardman Bard.

Writing a definitive history of beading on a loom is a job best left to historians and scholars. Here I would like to fill you in on a little history, then illustrate some events, styles, and techniques that relate to contemporary loomwork.

Beads have been made all over the world, but the seed beads we use for bead weaving originated mostly in Venice, Murano, and Bohemia, and are today manufactured mostly in Czechoslovakia and Japan.

The best-known examples of early glass bead weaving are Native American beadwork from the Great Lakes and Mid East areas, starting in the late eighteenth century, and the elegant purses from France and Austria, dating from the early eighteenth through the early twentieth centuries.

Bead weaving was also done in Africa where the time frame for its development roughly parallels the development of Native North American beadwork.

In North America, early bead weaving used shell beads which we call wampum. The earliest examples of shell beads were round flat disks, which were drilled with stone tools. A limited amount of wampum in the more desired tubular shape has been found in excavations dating to pre-European contact. This early wampum was extremely difficult to make using primitive drills made of wood, reed, or bone combined with abrasive cutting material such as sand, and was therefore highly valued.

The introduction of iron and steel tools from Europe allowed more precise drilling and easier production of wampum. Archeological excavations of early sites had small amounts of wampum. Increasing amounts of wampum beads were found in sites dating to about fifty years after the neighborhood went to hell (otherwise known as European contact). Factories were established in the colonies in the 1740s for the manufacture of wampum, and it was used in trade by whites and natives alike.

Several types of shells, notably periwinkle, whelk, conch, and large Quahog clamshells were used for wampum. The most highly prized purple beads were made from a portion of the Quahog shell. In addition to being strung as necklaces or other adornment, wampum beads were often woven into belts that recorded important events or commemorated important treaties.

Photograph by Martin Kilmer.

The beads for these purses were available in a wide variety of colors and the color finishes served to protect the beads from rust. This purse, probably from the late eighteenth or early nineteenth century, measures 7" × 11" plus fringe. From the collection of Martin Kilmer.

Photograph by Joe Coca.

This East African Maasai girl's apron appears to have been recycled from another use. The cord and binding on the brass chain are new material, possibly raffia, while the darker older fiber used as warp and weft is possibly jute. Note the woven selvedge at the ends of the loomwork. The warp appears to be two strands twined together. From the collection of David Castleberry.

Many materials were used for the warp and weft in wampum belts—nettle fiber, sinew, and leather strips, among others. Several styles of weaving were used, including the style shown below, which is similar to the method used in modern bead weaving.

Here is one of the methods used for weaving wampum belts.

While the story of buying Manhattan Island for twenty-four dollars worth of glass beads may not be true, many similar land purchases were made using manufactured wampum and glass beads. Unfortunately, the native people did not understand the European concept of owning or selling land.

Glass beads made their appearance in the Americas with the earliest European contact. In his 1492 logs at Samana Cay in the Bahamas, Columbus recorded giving beads to the "Indians." Subsequent European explorers and colonists used glass beads for trade—the brightly colored and easily useable beads were in great demand

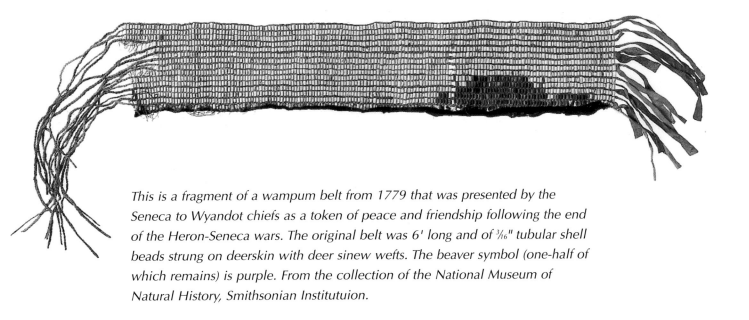

This is a fragment of a wampum belt from 1779 that was presented by the Seneca to Wyandot chiefs as a token of peace and friendship following the end of the Heron-Seneca wars. The original belt was 6' long and of ³⁄₁₆" tubular shell beads strung on deerskin with deer sinew wefts. The beaver symbol (one-half of which remains) is purple. From the collection of the National Museum of Natural History, Smithsonian Institutuion.

by the native peoples. East coast bead trading penetrated deep into the North American continent along the already well-developed intertribal trade routes, and later via French and English trappers and traders. Many beads also entered North America through the explorations of the Spanish conquistadors and missionaries. Robert Grey probably introduced glass beads to the West Coast in 1792 when he "discovered" the Columbia River and made contact with the Chinook people of the Lower Columbia region.

Native Americans began to use glass beads in place of many of the natural materials such as porcupine quills and shells that had previously been used for adornment.

At the beginning of the fifteenth century, a similar situation had occurred on the African continent. First, Arab traders had introduced glass beads from Persia and China along the Saharan trade routes, then Portuguese sea traders introduced European glass beads on the coast of West Africa. Also bearing beads, the Dutch, English, French

11

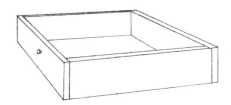

Box loom.

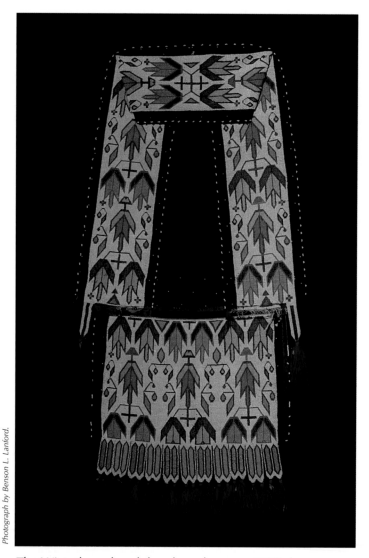

Photograph by Benson L. Lanford.

The Winnebago bandoleer bag above, c. 1875, has an overall length of 36¼", with a pouch of 12½" by 8¾" plus tabs and fringe; the strap is 4⅜" wide. It has classic features with the major motif repeated three times and the same elements repeated in the strap. The bag has geometric floral motif sand a swallowtail design.

and others followed these traders over the next hundred years.

The demand for trade beads was so great that the European bead industry prospered. In the mid-1800s advancements in manufacturing techniques in Venice and Bohemia made possible the production of tiny seed beads in bulk. As a result, hundreds of tons of seed beads per year were exported to both North America and Africa. The availability of many colors of small evenly-sized seed beads also promoted the forms of bead weaving that we are familiar with today.

Early Native American bead weavers used glass beads with weaving techniques previously used for wampum belts. Box and bow looms were used to some degree, but most work was done with tension warp weaving or loose warp weaving.

In tension warp weaving, the warp threads are attached at one end to a solid object such as a post or stake driven into the ground. The other end of the warp is attached to the weaver, possibly by tying the

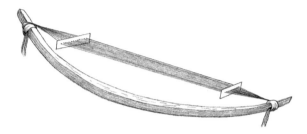

Bow loom.

warps to a peg tucked into a belt. The weaver's body controls the tension. A stiff piece of leather or bark with slots or holes separated and spaced the warp threads, and the weaver could simply roll up any unfinished work for easy transport.

Many variations of tension weaving styles have been roughly identified with specific tribal groups. Much early weaving in the Great Lakes area employed two weft threads with one needle above the warp and one below. The needles were reversed on alternate rows. This is the same method shown for wampum beads on page 10.

Loose warp weaving typically consisted of a cord strung between two solid points and warp threads tied with half hitches to this cord and hanging down loose as illustrated on page 14. A single or double weft could be used. An alternate method had beads strung on a double weft and the warp threads looped around the beads and hanging down. In both cases the weaver then added beads on the weft threads one at a

Photograph by Benson L. Lanford.

This Winnebago bandoleer bag, c. 1880, has an overall length of 33" and a pouch of 12¾ × 8" plus tabs and fringe; the strap is 4¼" wide. From the collection of Benson L. Lanford.

13

These garters, probably Chippewa, c. 1860, were tension warp or box loom woven and measure 11¼" × 2⅛". From the collection of Benson L. Lanford.

Typical setup for loose warp weaving.

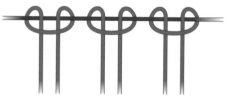

time using the fingers to manipulate the bead into place. A needle wasn't needed in either loose warp method. In some instances where double wefts were used the weaver would introduce a full or half twist into the weft thread between each warp. These methods were very time-consuming but created a firm, dense weave.

In time box looms became common and it is difficult to tell the difference between box loom weaving and tension warp weaving. The weaving techniques are the same; the only difference is the way the warp is held in tension.

The loose warp method was used to produce the pouches in the Winnebago bandoleer bags shown on pages 12 and 13. The straps on these bags were probably made using tension weave or a box loom. The garters in the photo above were also done with tension weave or a box loom.

Heddle weaving was probably introduced by French traders in the mid-1700s.

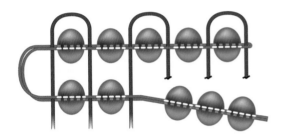

Alternate setup for loose warp weaving.

Examples of heddle weaving using yarn and pony beads have been dated to 1740. The heddle was used extensively by several Woodland tribes in the Great Lakes and Mideast areas. While we tend to think of heddle weaving in terms of looms, Native Americans used no special loom at all, instead employing the heddle in conjunction with either of the tight warp methods.

In setting up a loom with a heddle, alternate warp threads are strung either through the holes or through the slits. The heddle moves up and down, spearating the warp threads and forming a "shed." A bead-strung weft thread is passed through this shed. When the heddle is reversed, the weft thread is locked in place.

Photograph by Benson L. Lanford.

This hand carved heddle, possibly Winnebago, Potawatomi, or Mesquakie, is from the late nineteenth century and measures 3½" × 4½". From the collection Benson L. Lanford.

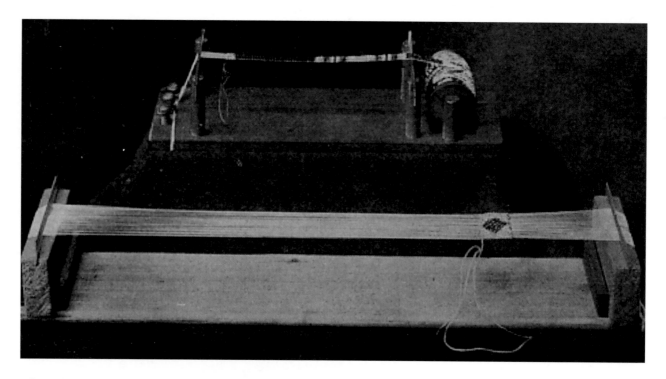

These looms, an "Apache" loom and a homemade version, appeared in the 1912 publication Priscilla Bead Work Book.

The Apache Bead Loom

The History of Beads by Helen Sherr Dubin shows an advertisement for the "Apache" bead loom circa 1910. As the Apache people were not known to do this type of bead weaving, it is likely that the maker of these looms was more interested in a snappy name than truth in advertising.

Small and wooden, the Apache loom resembles the small wire loom available in many bead weaving kits sold today and it is of the same basic type as the modern Miyuki looms from Japan.

The "Apache" loom sold for the princely sum of sixty cents. Or for two dollars you could get the loom, five bunches of beads, thread, twenty-five needles, and twenty-four patterns for "Indian Beading." This sounds like a bargain until you realize that two dollars was about a day's wage for the average worker in 1910.

The Apache loom ad suggests that a housewife can make pin money using the loom, and that it is good training for the mechanical or artistic development of small children. It is interesting to note that this and several other sources from the period refer to loom weaving as "Indian" beading.

The *Priscilla Bead Work Book,* published in 1912 and edited by Bell Robinson also shows an "Apache" loom along with a loom of her design. Her loom was made from available materials and very closely resembles the loom detailed in the next section of this book.

Also pictured in the Priscilla book are several French Woven Chain necklaces and the instructions for weaving them on the Apache loom. These necklaces are also referred to as Sautoir Chains by Sophie T. La Croix in *Old and New Designs in Beadwork* book number 20. Both the Priscilla book and the LaCroix book have been included in the Lacis Publication reprint called *Bead Work* (see bibliography).

I was lucky enough to borrow an original Apache loom from Jeanne Boardman Bard of Newport, Oregon whose shop includes a "Den of Antiquity." She also loaned me an original copy of the *Priscilla Bead Work Book.* I used the Apache loom to make the French Woven Chain necklace pictured on page 21, following the instructions in the article, which are reprinted on the following pages.

I wove the necklace using size A Nymo and Miyuki steel hex beads electroplated in 22k rose gold. The red accent beads are antique French cut metal beads.

I had some difficulty using this loom because it was designed for people with very small hands. Cutting all the warp threads to length and then trying to arrange individual threads across the spacing bars was frustrating. It was difficult to get all the warps in place and to maintain even tension. The working area on the loom is so short that the work has to be rolled over the take-up roll frequently, and this means loosening the warps and then trying to get them back straight and tight.

All in all, I find it much easier to use a "regular" loom with the techniques described in the next chapter.

The instructions for this necklace, which appear on the following pages, were originally published in The Priscilla Bead Work Book, *1912.*

FRENCH WOVEN CHAINS

The materials required in making these woven chains are a loom of the simplest type with a revolving spool at one end, beads, thread, a fine needle, and the pattern. A waist-length chain of about twelve beads in width requires usually seven bunches. The small French cut-steel beads make the daintiest chains, though small glass beads are also adaptable.

To set up your loom, cut strands of fine, strong silk about fifty inches long and of a color harmonizing with the beads or matching the outer rows; allow always one more strand than the number of beads in the width of design. Knot the warp threads together at one end and fasten around the brass nail in the revolving spool, wind about ten inches of the thread to be used later for medallion and fringe, and insert the brass peg in a hole on the end of the spool. Arrange the threads in the grooves on the first bridge, carry them over the length of the loom and through corresponding grooves on the second bridge, remove a peg at the bottom of the loom, draw the threads together through the hole and replace the peg.

To weave the chain, thread a length of fine sewing silk into a No. 12 needle. Hold the end of the thread in the left hand and the needle in the right and let the thread run under. Begin with the row of beads that comes next to the medallion, picking up the colors according to the pattern, press a single bead up into each space with the forefinger of the left hand, thread the needle back through each bead from right to left *over* the warp threads so that each bead is made secure in its groove. Having brought the thread out to the left, tie it to the end, which should be several inches long and which is later threaded into the needle, and run back and forth, through the beads. This is the only knot in the necklace, as ends are always secured by running through the beads already woven. Pass the needle from left to right under the warp and continue with the next row. For the strings between motifs, loosen the warp threads by removing the peg, divide the threads into pairs if the stringing is to be done that way, or use a single thread if preferred, and "string" enough beads to form strands of good spacing length between the motifs, usually from one and a half to twice the length of the motif. Alternate motifs and strings to within ten inches of the end of the warp threads.

To make the medallion, remove chain from the loom and rearrange with exact centre on the brass nail of the spool, taking care not to get the necklace twisted, wind the chain on the spool, bringing the two sides of the chain parallel a few inches above the lower bridge. A space is thus

19

formed which must be filled. Insert as many threads in the centre as there are extra beads in the medallion. Continue weaving across the entire width as in the small motifs. For the fringe, string beads to about the same length as medallion, and pass needle back through all except the end bead and fasten off by running thread into several rows of medallion. Or the fringe may be

divided into thirds and the threads drawn through small wooden button-molds strung with beads and fastened to cover the mold. If it is found difficult to thread the fine needle with the double threads for the stringing, the two threads may be waxed together at the ends and put through the beads without a needle.

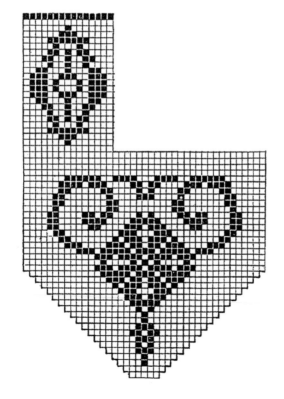

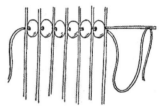

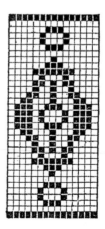

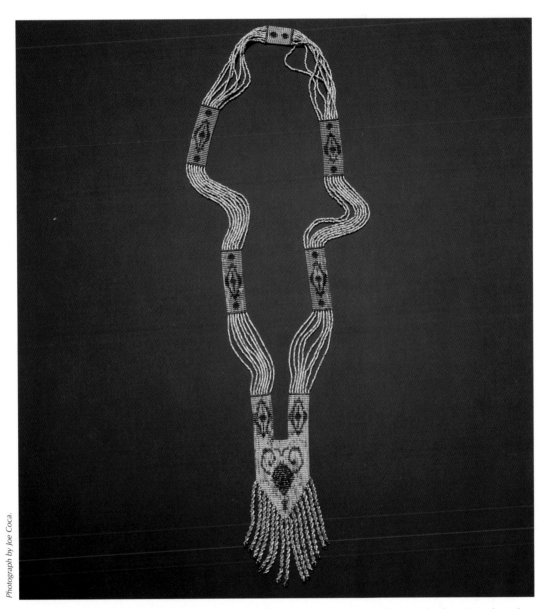

Photograph by Joe Coca.

Here is the chain I created from the Priscilla instructions. I used a total of 10,367 beads: Delica cut steel beads electroplated in 22k rose gold accented with antique French cut metal beads.

21

TOOLS AND TECHNIQUES FOR BEADING ON A LOOM

Using a simple loom, you can create fabric with thread as fixed warp and thread and beads as weft. The color and texture of the fabric is varied by bead choice, and the shape of the fabric is varied by the techniques used in weaving.

TOOLS AND MATERIALS

Looms

The loom is your basic tool. It does not need to be fancy or expensive. All that's required of a loom is that it hold warp threads under consistent tension while you weave. In fact, simplicity rules—the less "stuff" there is on the loom, the easier it is to use. Many looms are adjustable in length to match the size of the piece being woven; this saves on the amount of warp thread. I use a loom that sits on a flat surface, but some excellent looms stand vertically or at an angle. Probably no single loom meets every criterion for every type of project for every beadworker. Individuals should select or make a loom that suits their needs.

The loom I use bears a great resemblance to a basic loom pictured in the *Priscilla Bead Work Book* (see page 16). I prefer a flat base for stability and the flat surface is a handy place to keep beads and tools close at hand. End boards four inches high allow enough room to pass a hand under the warp threads. A simple sturdy spring serves to space the warp threads and to hold them in place during the warping process. Some looms use threaded rod or strung beads for spacers, but I find that these don't hold the warp threads firmly in place during warping.

Loom size will depend on the size of the work you intend to do. The small wire looms found in children's beading kits should be avoided because they do not have enough length or depth to allow easy working, and the spring coils are not tight enough to hold the warp threads while warping. However, these looms can be improved by carefully bending the ends up to a vertical position for additional length and vertical clearance.

An 8"× 38" loom is suitable for large neckpieces while a 4"× 20" loom is fine for pendants or other small projects. The 8"× 38" size was determined by a complex calculation of factors including the circumference of the earth, studies of the human anatomy by Leonardo de Vinci, and other secret formulae. It also happened to be the size of a piece of shelving material that I used to make my first loom, which I am still using.

Constructing a Basic Loom

The following are instructions for building a simple large loom. Remember that the dimensions can be changed to meet your individual needs. If you're planning a bracelet with a finished length of 7", you'll need a loom that will hold a 19" warp—7" for the weaving and 6" at each end for finishing. If you're planning a piece with fringe, you must also consider the length of the fringe.

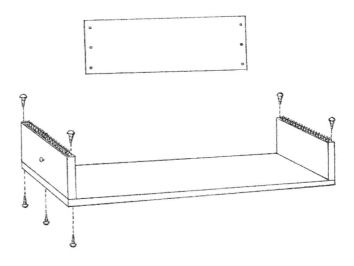

Construction plan for a basic loom.

Materials
- One 1"× 8" (¾"× 7¼" actual size) medium density fiberboard (MDF), 38" long. MDF is used for stability, and is available at most lumberyards. Pine or other wood may be substituted.
- Two 1"× 4" (¾ × 3½" actual size) pine cut 8" long.
- Two steel springs ¼" diameter by 5" long made of 30 to 40 gauge wire. When stretched to 7½", the springs will provide the right spacing for Delica beads. Larger, heavier springs and little wimpy springs do not work well. Springs of 30 to 40 gauge wire are available in several lengths at many hardware stores.
- Six 1½" deck screws.
- Four 1" size 6 round-head wood screws.
- Two ⅝" size 4 round-head wood screws.

Tools
- Saw for cutting the base and end pieces, unless the lumberyard will cut them for you.
- Square (if you're cutting the pieces yourself).
- Tape measure (if you're cutting the pieces yourself).
- Sandpaper, 100 grit.
- Electric drill.
- Size 8 countersink drill bit.
- ³⁄₃₂" drill bit.
- Phillips screwdriver.

23

Construction

Measure one base that is 8"× 38" from the MDF, and two end pieces that are each 4"× 8" from the 1"× 4" pine. Use the square to mark saw lines. Cut the pieces and sand the rough ends.

- Use the size 8 countersink bit to pre-drill three holes at each end of the base, as shown on page 23.
- Using the ³⁄₃₂" bit, pre-drill two holes in each of the 1"× 4" end boards as shown on page 23. Attach the springs to the end pieces with the 1" screws.
- Attach the end pieces to the base with the 1½" deck screws.
- Screw the ⅝" round-head screw into the end pieces as shown on page 23.

Thread

I use Nymo monocord for beading on a loom. It is a flat woven thread that resists twisting and is easier to thread on a needle than round woven thread. While some types of thread need to be waxed to reduce fraying, twisting, and knotting, waxing is not necessary with Nymo monocord. The most commonly used sizes range from 000 to FF, 000 being the thinnest. Sizes A or B are the most suitable sizes for loomwork with Delicas or other size 14° to 11° seed beads. Size 0 Nymo should be used for smaller beads or beads with smaller holes. I find that thread thinner than size 0 is too weak.

The weight of the thread used will affect the pliability and drape of the finished work. For a more pliable piece, use a thinner thread. I use the same weight for both warp and weft. For maximum strength, it generally is a good idea to use the heaviest weight thread possible.

Nymo is available in small bobbins and 100- or 300-yard spools; size B is readily available in 3500-yard 3-ounce spools. I buy the 3-ounce spools, and the cost of my thread in any project is very minor. Nymo is most commonly available in either black or white, but the small bobbins also come in a wide variety of colors. Thread that has been wound on these small bobbins comes off in tight coils, so give the thread a good stretch before you use it. The thread on the larger spools can come off in clumps and bunches, but putting a wide rubber band around the top end of the spool controls this. Commercially made net thread-covers also work, as, I am told, does the toe of a panty hose.

You can find a variety of colored size A Nymo in some fly-tying shops under the trade name Fishair. It comes in 100-yard spools.

I use black thread for almost everything. I do not use white thread unless I'm working with white or clear beads. Black thread recedes into the work, while white thread is very visible and can dominate the beads. Colored thread can influence the shading of a design, especially if you are using transparent beads. Another area where thread color is important is when you're using very small seed beads. In this case, thread color becomes a definite design factor because the thread shows between small beads more than it does between larger beads. White thread may be colored with colorfast felt-tip marking pens.

In any loomworked piece, the thread is most visible at the edges. Again, you may use a colorfast felt-tip marking pen once the beading is complete.

Beads

Miyuki Delica and Toho Antique Beads

These Japanese cylindrical beads are interchangeable and come in a wide variety of colors and finishes—it is impossible to find as wide a color palette in any other type of bead. Really big holes make it easy to pass a needle and thread through them several times. Delicas and Tohos work well for weaving and create a very smooth fabric.

Delicas are almost square in aspect, nearly as wide as they are tall. These beads are very regular in size, but they are not perfect—some culling is necessary. There is also a slight size difference between the standard Delicas and the five-sided hex beads commonly called "cuts," and some very slight size differences between beads with different finishes.

Japanese Seed Beads

These are available in many colors, are fairly regular in size, but are oval in aspect, taller than they are wide. They come in sizes 11° and 15°. Also available are two-cuts in size 11° and hex cuts in size 15°. These are both more square in aspect, have large holes, and work well for weaving.

Czech Seed and Cut Beads

These traditional beads come in a wide variety of colors and finishes, and many vintage and antique varieties are available. The sizes most readily available range from 22° to 9°. Sizes 11° and 12° are most commonly used for loom weaving. Czech seed beads are more oval in aspect, while cut beads are more square in aspect, like Delicas.

You must use great care in matching sizes; there is a lot of variation within a given size in both diameter and width. Using any bead smaller than size 14° can be hazardous to your mental health. Hole size in the small beads can be a major loomwork problem because you have to make many thread passes through every bead.

With any type of bead it is necessary to cull out the uneven and under- or over-sized beads. Uneven beads should be discarded; under- and oversized-beads can be used in fringe or other embellishment.

It is important to use beads of consistent size in a project. Mixing beads of varying widths can cause waviness in the body and uneven edges. Pick a median size and try to stick to it. The size of the outside beads in any row is most important and you may have to use a smaller or larger bead to keep the outside edges straight.

Many bead finishes are not permanent. Some coated, galvanized, or dyed beads will fade or the finishes will rub off. These and other problems are covered in Virginia Blakelock's *Those Bad Bad Beads* and in *The Beader's Companion* by Judith Durant and Jean Campbell (see bibliography).

In *Those Bad Bad Beads*, Virginia suggests testing beads in bleach to see if they are colorfast. Your concern for this problem will depend somewhat on your use of the beads. A bead surface that rubs off with hard use may not be a problem in a wall hanging, while a bead that fades in sunlight may be. On the other hand, beads that fade in sunlight won't be a problem in a necklace unless you wear it sunbathing.

If you just can't stand it and have to use one of the less durable beads in a piece that will be handled, you can coat the beads or the finished work with clear Krylon spray, available from art supply stores. I have done this on finished work with no detrimental change in appearance.

Suzanne Cooper, author of many bead books, suggests putting loose beads in a Ziploc bag and spraying one or two short bursts of clear Krylon into the bag, sealing it, then scrunching the beads around to coat them. Scrunch the bag again after the spray has dried to separate any beads that have stuck together.

Graph Paper

When you are doing a complicated design with many colors, I recommend that you chart the design on graph paper and work from the chart. The true-scale graph papers provided on pages 107–110 may be enlarged or reduced to meet your needs. I use a copy machine to create large sheets with squares big enough to see easily. Be sure to choose the proper graph for the bead type you are using.

Computer design programs generate graphs that can be printed, and *A Beadworker's Tool Book* by Pam Preslar is an excellent source of graph paper for many types of beads and beadwork.

Needles

For Delicas or size 11° to 14° seed or cut beads, use size 12 needles. I prefer the standard beading needle, but the longer Japanese beading needles are fine. For finishing that involves sewing in short threads, use the short size 12 sharps. If these are not readily available, carefully cut a regular beading needle back to about an inch long and file the cut end to a smooth rounded point.

To avoid spearing warp threads while weaving, some people blunt the ends of their regular beading needles by carefully clipping the point off, then smoothing the end with a fine file or emery paper. On the other hand, a sharp needle keeps you alert.

If you are using small beads, use small needles. Size 16 are the smallest needles available but they are hard to find in stores.

Scissors

Use small scissors with a very fine point for trimming threads close to beads.

Light

Good light is imperative; it will protect your eyesight. Full spectrum lights such as the Ott light are available in many bead stores or by mail order. Full-spectrum incandescent and fluorescent lights are good, as are quartz Halogen lights, but the latter generate excess heat. Light from two sources is ideal, and you always need enough to see the needle as it passes between beads while weaving. Color-correct light can help when you're determining colors, but I prefer making critical color choices in daylight.

Magnifier

If you need one. Some people find that inexpensive drugstore reading glasses work fine. Please don't be vain about using a magnifier; beading is a lot more fun when you can see the holes.

Straightedge or Ruler

Use a ruler for measuring. Push the straight edge against each row as you finish to keep rows straight and even.

Bead Trays

Many types of trays and containers may be used to hold working beads. Plastic petrie and other small dishes work very well. The container should be sufficiently wide and shallow to allow you to pick up multiple beads without having them fall back into the container.

Many beaders simply pour out small piles of beads onto a piece of soft leather or cloth. In this case the small triangular metal scoops available in most bead stores are useful for picking up unused beads. These scoops also make good bead trays. Plastic containers and their lids can also be used. Porcelain watercolor dishes hold nine colors in a small space and are quite stable, but I have a little trouble picking up beads from the small depressions.

Adhesives

Use a thick contact adhesive such as E-6000 or barge cement to glue beadwork when bleed-through would be a problem.

Fray Check or Clear Nail Polish

These work for repairing frayed threads. Also use them for sealing knots or threads in woven selvedge.

Time

In today's busy world, time is our most valuable commodity. For this reason it doesn't make sense to fuss about minor differences in the cost of beads and threads and the like. Use the best that you can afford and make your time count. By the same token, give yourself quality time and make the most of your materials.

Working Environment

It is important to have comfortable working conditions. A comfortable and supportive chair and a table of the right height are essential. If you are experiencing back pain or muscle strain while working, you need to change something. Do not try to work for long periods without a break. Get up, stretch, relax, and loosen up. It is also important to change your eye focus periodically by stopping and looking at something far away and letting your eyes refocus to normal.

TECHNIQUES

In this chapter I'll give you the basic techniques of warping, weaving, and finishing. Then we'll get to the nitty-gritty of designing and planning a project and having some fun.

Warping the Loom

This does not mean leaving it out in the rain.

You will always need one more warp thread than the number of beads wide the project is—one bead is placed between each pair of warp threads. If the project ends in a one-bead point, there must be an even number of warp threads to accommodate an odd number of beads.

Using a simple overhand loop knot, tie off the warp thread to the screw at one end of the loom. Starting at approximately the center of the loom, string the warp thread over and between two coils of the spacing spring. Holding the warp thread taut, but without stretching it, go over and between

Use a simple overhand loop knot to tie warp thread to the screw at one end of the loom.

two corresponding center coils of the spacing spring at the other end of the loom. Go around the screw and return, using the slot next to the one used first. Repeat until you have the required number of warps on the loom. It is not necessary to follow any set pattern when adding threads, but the warps should stay centered on the loom and parallel to each other.

The spacing of the warp threads in the coils of the spacing spring will depend on the width of the beads you are using. You can vary the thread spacing to match the beads; do this by skipping some coils or by placing two warp threads in some coils.

To check the warp thread spacing for the beads you are using, put ten warp threads on the loom and then put nine beads on a needle and hold them under the warp threads. Press the beads up between the warp threads to see how they fit and adjust accordingly. The spacing does not have to be exact, and slightly wide spacing is better than narrow spacing.

Keep the tension on all the threads the same. The warp threads should be tight, but not too tight. If you can play the strings like a violin, they are probably too tight. On the other hand, they should not sag like Aunt Martha's clothesline. If you do end up with warp threads stretched too tight the piece will bunch up when you cut it loose from the loom. When this happens, place the

Warp threads should be centered on the loom and parallel to each other.

piece on a flat surface and pet it and roll the beads to help the warp threads move around and relieve the tension. This technique may not work on large pieces or if you have speared a lot of warp threads while weaving.

Basic Weaving Techniques

My instructions are written for right-handed people working with the loom flat on the table and parallel to the body, i.e. the warp is running left to right. Right-handers usually work from the near side of the loom to the far side, tying on to the near side. Subsequent rows are added to the right of the first row. Lefties would work in the other direction; subsequent rows are added to the left of the first row. If you are left-handed or prefer to have the loom vertical to your body, i.e. the warp is running straight out from the body, you can easily adapt the instructions.

To begin, cut a weft thread about four or five feet long. Later you may want to use longer weft threads.

How to thread a needle

Trim the thread to a smooth, slightly tapered end. Hold the thread between your left thumb and index finger, with just the point of the thread showing. Bring the eye of the needle down onto the thread. As the thread enters the eye of the needle roll the finger and thumb apart to allow the thread to go on through.

If you have a frayed thread end and not enough thread for cutting back to a solid area, coat the end with nail polish or Fray Check and press the thread with your fingers to form a flat end. After it dries, trim a smooth point with scissors and thread in the normal way.

Weaving a Piece with a Squared or Straight End

Once the loom is warped with the required number of threads, tie the weft thread to the outside warp thread at the near side of the loom with a single overhand knot. Leave a 5" to 6" tail, which will be sewn in later. Be sure to tie far enough from the end of the loom to allow for fringe, if any, and finishing.

Thread on the proper number and colors of beads for the first row. Pass the needle under all the warp threads, and pull the

Tie a weft thread to the outside warp with a single overhand knot.

weft thread through until the beads are in place under the warp threads. Holding gentle tension on the weft thread with the right hand, use the index finger of the left hand to press as many of the beads up between the warp threads as possible, starting from the far side and working back to the near. Make sure that there is one bead between each pair of warp threads. Now pass the needle back through the beads that are in position. Be sure to keep the needle *above* the warp threads, and do not spear any of the warp threads. Do not try to do more than a few beads at a time. Be happy with even two or three at a time. This is not a contest.

Once the needle point is through as many beads as are in place, pause with the needle in the work, relax, take a breath, and then press up a few more beads and continue as before until all the beads in the first row are in place. If the piece is wider than the length of your needle, pull the needle on through, but only far enough to get enough slack to re-enter. Do not pull all of the weft thread through until the row is completed. Before you pull the needle through and out of the work, check to make sure that you have not inadvertently missed any beads or gone *under* any warp threads. Do this by pressing up on the threads ahead of the row while the needle is in place and see if any warps pop up above the beads.

If you messed up on this first row, do not rip the row out. Leave the bad row in place and repeat it, doing it right. Having the beads in place in the bad row establishes the proper spacing of the warp threads and will help in getting the next row done properly. After doing a few rows, you can untie the initial knot and remove the bad row.

Now thread on the proper number and colors of beads for the second row. Pass the needle under the warp threads and pull the weft thread through as for the first row. But for this and subsequent rows, press the beads up into place starting from the near side rather than from the far as in the first row. Use a gentle rocking or rolling motion with your fingers to encourage the beads to pop up between the warp threads. As you press the beads into place, check for the right color and number of beads. This time beads should stay in place. Press up on the beads with the index finger of the left hand to keep the beads as far above the warp

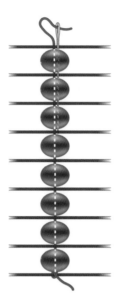

Making sure there is one bead between each pair of warp threads, pass the needle back through the first row.

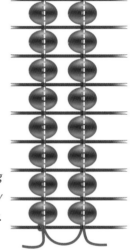

Keep the tension snug and consistent from row to row.

threads as possible. Pass the needle back through the beads, again making sure the needle passes *above* the warp threads. After passing through all the beads, pull the weft thread almost all the way through, leaving a small loop on the far side. Pull on this loop to remove any slack in the bottom weft thread, then pull the weft thread through snugly. The tension on the weft thread is important to keeping the edge even and the piece smooth. The tension should be snug and consistent from row to row. Continue until all rows are completed.

31

Increasing and Decreasing

Increasing and decreasing are two basic techniques that confuse and bewilder many people. Fear not! It is really quite simple.

There are two main things involved in both increasing and decreasing. First, you must secure both the old outside warp thread and the new outside warp thread. Secondly, you must position the weft thread for the next row of beading.

I am showing you the methods that work best under every circumstance. Do not shortcut! Skipping one of the steps will anger the bead gods and cause your needle to break off. Increasing or decreasing with a method that leaves thread exposed or the first bead improperly positioned results in shoddy-looking work.

Increasing

Step 1: Do a full wrap of the old, or current, outside warp thread, ending with the weft thread coming out toward you.

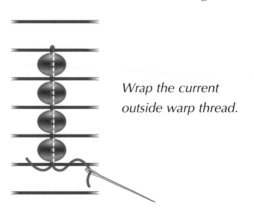

Wrap the current outside warp thread.

Step 2: Pick up a new bead, and slide the bead up the weft thread and into position next to the old outside warp thread. Hold the bead in position with the thumb and forefinger of the left hand.

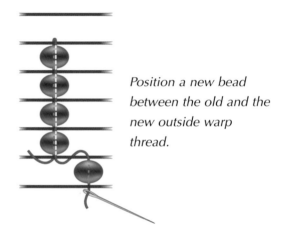

Position a new bead between the old and the new outside warp thread.

Step 3: Bring the needle around and over the top of the new outside warp thread, through the bead, and under the old outside warp thread. Pull the weft thread through to secure the new bead in place.

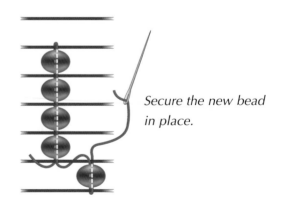

Secure the new bead in place.

Continue holding the bead with the thumb and forefinger until you complete this operation to prevent the bead from sliding up the warp threads or falling out of place.

A common problem in this step is incorporating more than one new warp thread. Make sure that the other warp threads are held back out of the way, and that you only go around one.

Step 4: Pick up the rest of the beads for the row and complete the row in the normal manner. Do nothing extra on the other side, except to add the right number of beads.

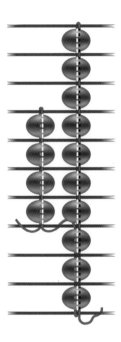

Use the same method to increase by more than one bead.

Complete the row in the usual manner.

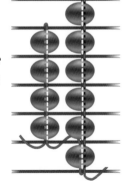

Increasing by More than One Bead

Use the same technique outlined above, except that in Step 2 add multiple beads, and in Step 3 pull the needle through all the added beads.

Decreasing

Step 1: Pass the needle around and over the top of the old outside warp thread, and then pass the needle through the outside bead. Pull the weft thread through and tug gently to avoid a loop at point A.

Wrap the outside warp thread and pass back through the outside bead.

A

33

Step 2: Pass the needle down in front of the new outside warp thread. Do a full wrap of the new outside warp thread, ending with the weft thread under the warp.

Wrap the new outside warp thread.

Step 3: Add all the beads for the new row and complete the row in the normal manner. Do nothing extra on the other side, except to decrease the right number of beads.

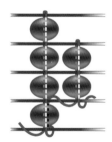

Complete the row in the usual manner.

Decreasing by More than One Bead
Use the same technique as for a single-bead decrease, except that in Step 1, pass the needle through as many beads as the decrease desired.

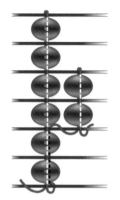

Use the same method to decrease by more than one bead.

Weaving Triangles
The techniques for weaving triangles are the same as for a square end start except for a few things. Some people find increasing more difficult than decreasing and recommend starting a triangular piece at the wide end. I feel that the difference in difficulty between increasing and decreasing is minor and recommend starting at the pointed end for a few reasons.

Starting the longest row on a very wide piece can be very frustrating, especially if the warp thread spacing is not perfect. On the other hand, if you start at the pointed end, you will only need to put on about twenty to twenty-five warp threads to start, adding others as you need them. If there is any problem with the spacing, you can make adjustments when you add these additional warp threads.

Another advantage to starting at the pointed end is that you will not have to work around all the extra warp threads. You also don't have to worry about starting with the exact center pair of warp threads—you can center up when you add additional warp threads.

Rather than start at the one-bead end of the work, start at the first five-bead row. Starting with fewer than five beads can be difficult because narrow work has a tendency to flip over and twist the warp threads. Tie a weft thread on the near side of the center pair of warps as far from the end of the loom as necessary to leave enough warp thread for finishing each end of the piece. Leave a twelve-inch tail of weft thread to use later to finish the point. Proceed weaving as you would for a square-end start, increasing as necessary to shape the triangle.

Ending and Adding Weft Threads

To knot or not to knot, that is the question. Some beaders finish their weft threads without knots by running the thread back and forth through the work and counting on friction to hold it in place. This works okay for beads with small holes. However, when you're using beads with large holes such as Delicas this is a questionable method, and one that I avoid in any case.

I prefer to use a secure knot to anchor the thread ends into the work. A secure knot involves the warp thread and both weft threads at the juncture where the knot is being made.

Ending A Weft

When the weft thread is too short to complete another row, sew it back into the work. There are two methods of doing this.

Method One: If you haven't ended on an increase row you may take the needle back into the previous row, pass through several beads, tie an overhand knot (making sure to incorporate the warp thread and both weft threads), and pull the thread tight. Pass the needle through several more beads, then out of the work. Pull tight again and the knot will disappear inside the beads. Try not to exit the work at the outside edge; if you do you will be trimming next to the outside warp, which is dangerous. Do not

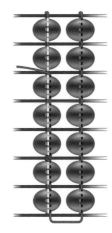

Pass through several beads, tie an overhand knot, and pass through several more beads.

trim off the weft thread end yet. Leave it and trim it flush with the beads later. The reason for this is that you may need to sew other threads through this same spot and if you have trimmed flush you may inadvertently dislodge the end of the thread that you have previously trimmed. It is better to wait until all the threads have been buried in any given area before trimming any off flush with the beads.

Method Two: If you have ended on an increase row, pass the needle around the outside warp and back through the top of the beads as described in Step 1 of Decreasing (see page 33). Then proceed as in Method One.

Adding a Weft

Weft threads can be added by two methods.

Method One: Tie the new weft thread to the outside warp thread with a simple overhand knot, just as you did for the first weft thread. Leave a 5" to 6" tail hanging or tape it back out of the way. You will sew the tail into the work later.

Method Two: Introduce the new weft thread into the just completed row, or into the previous row. Tie it off and bring it out of the edge of the work toward you and proceed weaving as usual. With this method, the weft is already tied in and

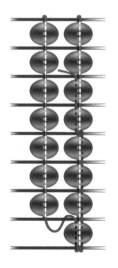

Wrap thread around outside warp and back through the top of the beads.

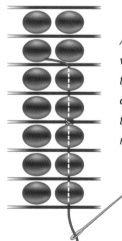

Add a new weft thread to the row just completed or the previous row.

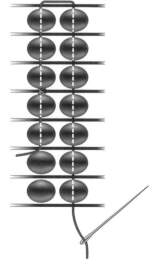

the tail is out of the way. As before, do not trim the tail flush at this time.

Finishing Techniques

Once you have finished the weaving and have the loose weft thread tails sewn in, you are ready to remove the work from the loom. Make absolutely sure that you are ready! Remember that you must leave enough warp thread at either end for sewing in or fringing and then sewing in; you can cut right next to the end screws if you need the extra length. Now, go ahead and cut that sucker loose.

Sewing in Warp Threads

This is another spot where new weavers panic or lose interest, but never fear; while it can get a tad tedious to finish off the ends, it is not difficult.

If you're working with beads that have small holes, it may not be necessary to knot the warp thread ends as you weave them in, but only to reverse direction at least once, depending on friction to secure them. However, I prefer to knot the warp thread ends securely into the work. Whichever method you employ, the important thing is to secure all threads and hide the ends in the rows of beads.

If you're going to sew the end of the loom work down to a backing, or wrap it around a bar or tube, you don't have to knot the warp ends as they are sewn in. The backing or wrapping will secure them.

Finishing Square-End Warp Threads

On the square end of a piece it will be impossible to hide all of the warp ends in the first row of beads, so you will thread the warp ends up into the piece by going between the beads and weft threads.

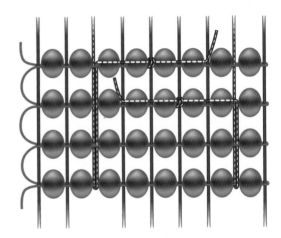

Sew the warp threads into the piece by weaving between the beads and weft threads.

To avoid passing through areas with lots of crossed threads and knots, follow a pattern and sew in first threads that go the farthest. For instance, if a piece is fifty beads wide, take every fifth thread up to the seventh row, then every fourth thread up to the sixth row, and so on. The idea is to spread the weaving in over a large area and avoid passing too many threads through one row

37

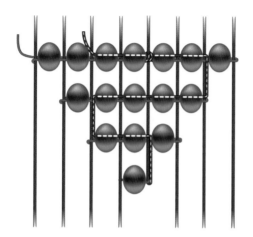

Knot in a row containing at least seven beads.

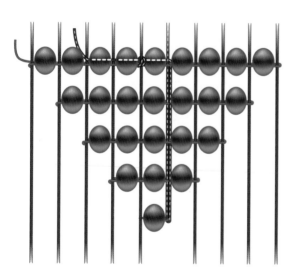

Weave some of the warp ends farther into the piece by going between the beads and weft threads.

of beads. Some stiffness is inevitable, but spreading out the thread and any knots you may use can minimize it.

Finishing Pointed-End Warp Threads

The most difficult warp threads to sew in are those at the end of a pointed-end piece. Do these first, using one of two techniques.

Weave the warp thread back and forth through the rows of beads until you have enough space to tie a secure knot. Generally it is desirable to knot in a row at least seven beads wide.

If you weave all the warp threads with this back and forth method, the holes in the beads of the first few rows will become overcrowded. For this reason, weave some of the warp ends farther into the work by going between the beads and weft threads until you have enough space to tie a knot.

Selvedge Ends

If work is to be sewn to a backing or folded back on itself and sewn down, you can create a selvedge edge by weaving the weft thread back and forth through the warp threads. Take care to keep the tension constant so the work won't pucker up. Weave at least ¼ inch of selvedge, tying in a fresh weft at either end of the work as necessary. To end the last weft thread, weave it over, under, over, under at least four previous weft threads. When completed, apply Fray Check to the selvedge threads and allow to dry. Glued together, the warp threads can then be cut, and the

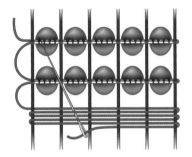

Create a selvedge end for pieces that will be sewn to a backing.

selvedge can be folded under when the work is sewn to the backing material or sewn back onto itself.

Correcting Mistakes

A common problem is missed warp threads. Check each row as you finish to make sure that you missed no warp threads. Press up on the warp threads ahead of the row. It is best to check while the needle is still in place. If you have missed one or more warp threads, correct the problem now. If you don't detect missed warp threads until later, you can correct them by running a fresh weft thread over the missed warp. You may use any tail that is going to be sewn in or you may introduce an additional thread to sew over the skipped spot. You can do this anytime, even after the piece is off the loom. I have discovered missed warps months after finishing a piece.

Another problem is speared warps. You can check for this by gently sliding the row up the warps just before you snug it in place. Speared threads will prevent the beads from sliding up between the warp threads. Speared warps can be a problem if you wish to pull the warp thread through the work later. To correct the problem, remove the thread from the needle and pull it back through the row. Rethread the needle and pass back through the beads without spearing warp threads.

DESIGNING AND ADVANCED TECHNIQUES

I can see it in my head but. . . I often refer to the design process as the What-ifs and the How-tos. I may say, what if I do this, how will it look, or how do I do this to get the effect I want? Most of this discussion on designing will deal with my specialty, neckpieces, but the principles apply to all types of loomwork.

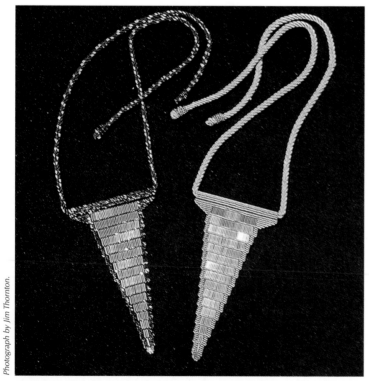

Photograph by Jim Thornton.

Trans America Tower—Day & Night. 2" × 6".

THE WHAT-IFS

Each of us possesses a perception of beauty, proportion, and design, and we create beauty in our everyday lives. When we focus those perceptions, we create art.

Every artist or craftsperson draws from the things around them, or from visions in their head. I see necklaces in architecture as in the Trans American Tower shown at left. I can turn a building upside down and find a necklace. Architectural details may provide a design idea. The Chrysler building in New York City is a good example. There are literally hundreds of art deco designs in that one building.

Ads and photos in magazines will often suggest a shape or color combination. Graphic artists get paid big bucks for creating color and design combinations that are pleasing or attention getting. It is a major no-no to steal somebody else's design, but often just the suggestion of a shape or color combination will trigger a design. The necklace shown at right was inspired and derived from a photo of the entrance to an art deco building in Miami. Whenever I see something that inspires me I save it and file it away in my idea box.

Sometimes just purchasing a new bead will trigger a design idea.

Very often it is possible or desirable to reduce a complex object to basic forms and produce an impression of that object. This may mean eliminating many details but keeping the feel of the thing being depicted.

The use of bold colors and shapes can be very effective, and very dramatic.

You just have to open your mind and let the ideas come in. It helps to have a weird or twisted imagination and to be somewhat compulsive.

Once I visualize what I think a neck-piece will look like and what effect I want to achieve, I may do a rough sketch, and if the shapes and details are simple I am ready to start. However, if the shapes and details are complex, it will be necessary to graph the design bead by bead.

An excellent source of designs are needlepoint and cross-stitch patterns. These have the added bonus of being already graphed out. But because these graphs are square, when you translate the designs into beads the result will be vertically elongated. This distortion will be less with Delica and Czech three-cut beads than with seed beads. For the necklace shown on page 44 I used a Berliner needlepoint graph.

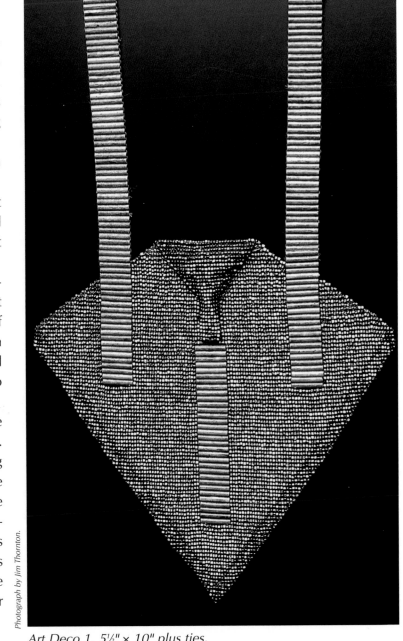

Photograph by Jim Thornton.

Art Deco 1. 5½" × 10" plus ties.

41

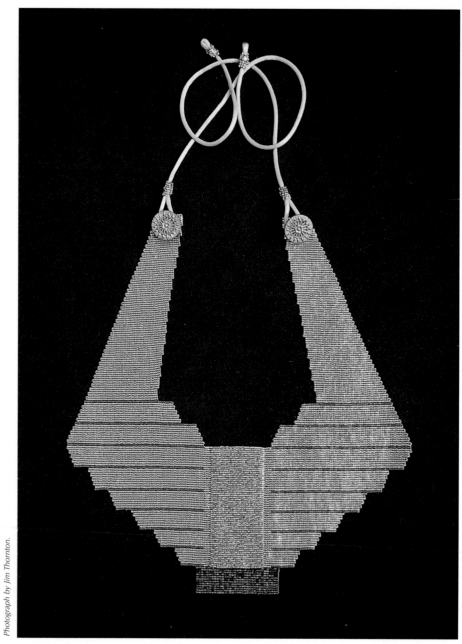

Photograph by Jim Thornton.

El Castillo Gold. 12" × 14".

Photograph by Jim Thornton.

Art Deco 4. 6" × 18".

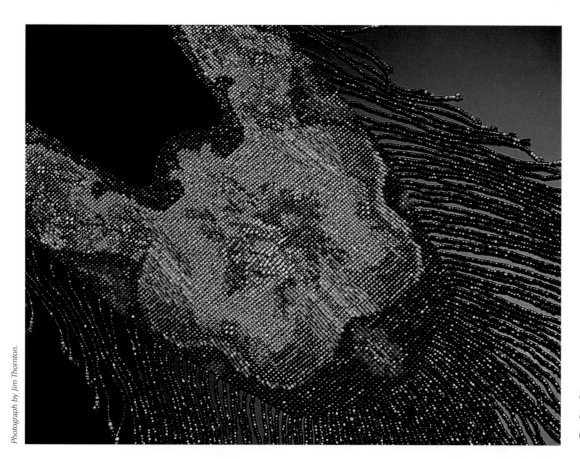

Photograph by Jim Thornton.

*Berliner
Needlepoint.
6½" × 18".*

THE HOW-TOS

For any design idea you must consider the techniques involved. You must first determine if the design is feasible. Can it be done in beads? Can it be done on the loom? What kind and type of beads will work best? Many a "good" idea will prove to be undoable on the loom, or better done in some other type of beadwork.

There are several things to consider before starting a project, the first being whether or not it will fit on your loom. How long will your finished piece be? Will it have fringe? If so, how long will the fringe be? If you're making a neckpiece, how long will the straps be? Considering these factors, will your loom be big enough? Keep in mind that you will need an extra 5" to 6" at each end of warp thread for finishing; measure the warp thread all the way to the wrap around the screws at the ends of the loom.

Limitations of Beading on A Loom

Detail

The amount of detail possible will depend on the size of the beads and the scale of the piece. Very fine detail is difficult to achieve. Using smaller beads or making the piece larger may be the solution.

Curves

Curves and circles are difficult unless the scale of the design is large. Keep in mind that what looks clunky on large-scale graph paper will probably look better when actually done in beads. Try graphing on true-size graph paper to get an idea of how it will look. Most curves work better if they are in orderly progressions. Curves should be smooth and not herky-jerky.

Angles

Angles in loomwork are restricted to regular progressions such as one to one or two to one, i.e. increase or decrease one bead per row, two beads per row, etc. Irregular progressions do not look good.

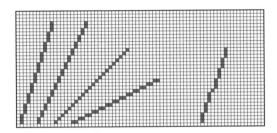

The angles at left work well because of their orderly progressions. The irregular progression at right looks more jagged than linear.

Planning for Size and Weight of Neckpieces

In designing loomwork in general and neckpieces in particular, the piece must be structured to support the weight of the beads. This is especially true when doing split loom straps that are woven as part of the necklace. If there is too much weight in relation to the size and shape of the piece, either in terms of fringe, large beads incorporated into the piece, or the loomwork itself, then the piece may collapse. The Pastel Peacock neckpiece shown on page 46 needs more loomworked material at points

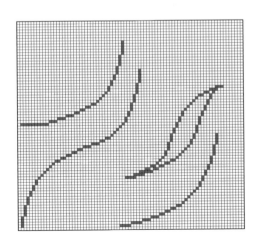

When plotting curves, fill in each square of the graph to ensure they are in orderly progression.

A and B to give it enough body to support the weight of the fringe.

The structure of the necklace shown at right does an excellent job of distributing the weight of a heavy bead through the loomwork.

Using metal bars, rods, and tubes is an interesting way of adding support to a necklace and allowing the use of heavy feature beads and other design features that otherwise would not hang properly.

The necklace I call Construction shown on page 48 shows the use of a metal rod. The loomworked pendant and the straps are sewn around the bar, and to each other.

Lady Face on page 49 shows the use of a metal tube with the loomworked pendant wrapped and sewn around the tube. The strap in this small necklace is a braided cord.

The Golden Drape neckpiece on page 50 utilizes a flat metal bar sewn into the loomwork as support.

The Double Flap necklace shown on page 51 has the loomwork enclosing a ¼-inch square tube. The front triangle hangs ¼ inch in front of the back triangle, giving the piece added depth.

Split Loom Straps

To weave split loom straps, you work the body first, then continue up the strap on the

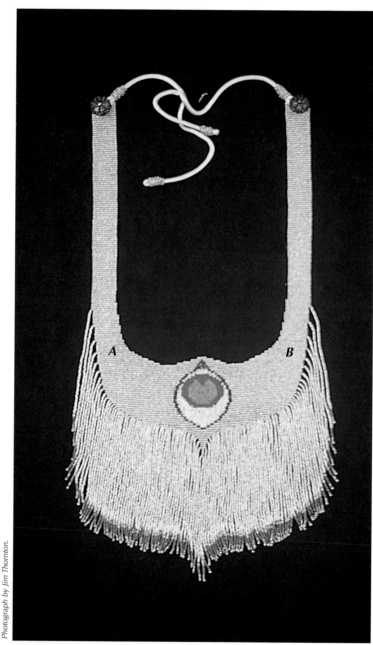

Photograph by Jim Thornton.

46   *Pastel Peacock. 8" × 18" plus ties.*

near side, turn the loom, and weave the strap on the other side.

Neck Width

You must consider how a neckpiece will hang on the body. Average neck width, or the distance between the straps, should be about four inches. The Pastel Peacock necklace shown at left is six inches between the straps. Reducing this dimension to about four inches would help the piece hang properly.

Too little space between the straps can make the straps deform as they spread to go around the neck. This will be particularly noticeable on a necklace with wide and/or short straps. One solution to this problem is to use non-loomworked straps such as strung beads, braided cord, or rattail.

You may also include sections of strung beads in the straps. This allows the strap to shape itself to any neck width. When working on the loom, these beads have to be strung on the warp threads while warping the loom, so you'll have to plan ahead as for the French Chain in the first chapter.

Strap Length

If you are designing for your own use you may make the strap length to suit your own needs. If, however you are not aware of whom the wearer will be or you want the necklace to be adjustable, you might use

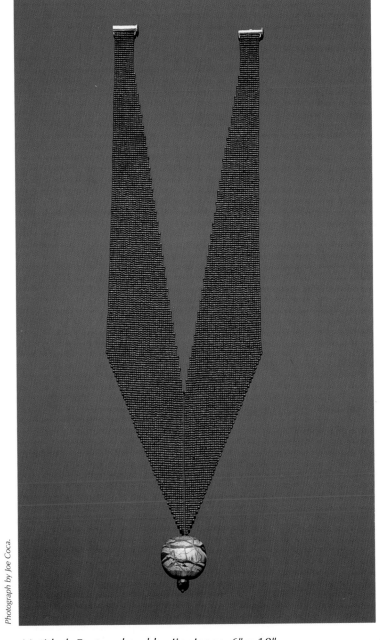

Photograph by Joe Coca.

Untitled. Feature bead by Jim Jones. 6" × 18".

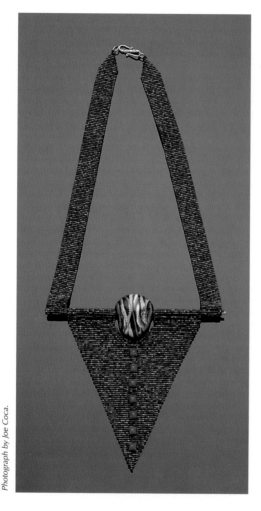

Photograph by Joe Coca.

Construction. Feature bead by Jim Jones. 6" × 12".

of the straps. The length of the closure needs to be considered in determining the strap length.

It is a good idea to pick your closure before the strap is woven. The shaping of the end of the strap will depend on the type of closure, or conversely the type of closure will determine the shaping of the end of the strap. Some closures attach to a single- or double-bead point while others attach to a square end.

Bead Counts

When designing beadwork you'll need to know how many beads per inch there are for the bead size that you are using.

In calculating how many beads it takes to weave one inch in width you must consider the warp threads between every bead. Once you have determined the beads per inch you can determine how many beads high and wide your design will be.

The following bead counts are based on using size B Nymo warp thread.

Delicas 17 beads per inch in width, 15 beads per inch in height.

Japanese size 11 seed beads 16 beads per inch in width, 12 beads per inch in height.

Japanese size 15 seed beads 26 beads per inch in width, 15 beads per inch in height.

Czech size 12 seed beads 17 beads per inch in width, 15 beads per inch in height.

Because of the variations in actual size of

ties of woven cord or rattail. Adjustable ties make a necklace much more versatile. Otherwise, I find that about twelve inches is a good length for most loomworked straps.

Closures

The type of closure you use will influence the strap width and the shaping of the end many beads, you will have to experiment to get accurate bead counts. *The Beader's Companion* (see Bibliography) is an excellent reference for additional information.

Graphing

Whether you are graphing your design on true-scale or large-scale graph paper, you must remember that each square represents one bead, and your design must be laid out square by square.

True-scale graphing can be useful when you want to know the actual size of the finished piece. I find it easier to do the actual beadwork working from a large-scale graph. I use a copy machine to enlarge graph paper to ⅛" squares on sheets that measure 11" × 17". For large designs I tape together two or more sheets in order to graph out as much of the piece as is necessary.

Transparent graph sheets can be made on a copy machine and true-size sheets can be laid over a picture or an object to convert it to colored squares. You can make one transparent graph for each type and size of bead that you normally use.

Do not do unnecessary graphing! For a very simple piece, you may not need to graph at all. For symmetrical pieces, graph only half the design. If a design is very complex with lots of color and pattern changes, I write out the bead sequence, row by row, as follows.

Lady Face.
3" × 4" plus ties.

Photograph by Martin Kilmer.

Row 1: 4 pink, 7 blue, 8 black, 16 red, 4 puce.

Row 2: 6 pink, 8 puce, 4 black, 12 mauve, 9 black.

And so on.

It's a good idea to write up all the rows at one sitting when you can concentrate. Using this system makes it possible to work faster and avoid mistakes when you get to the actual weaving—you don't have to take time to rethink and count every time you return to the work.

Photograph by Martin Kilmer.

Golden Drape. 6" × 18".

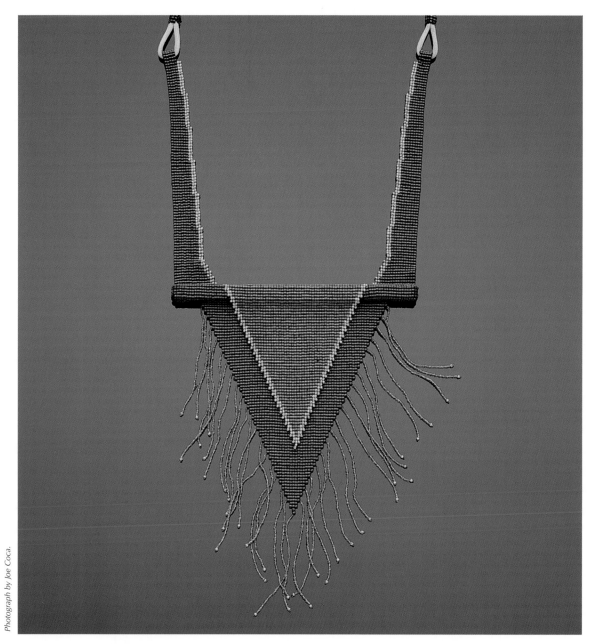

Double Flap. 5¾" × 14" plus ties.

Designing on the Computer

There are several programs available that will allow you to graph a design, color it in bead by bead, and get a row by row printout of the entire piece. While I don't work with them, I am told that these computer programs are relatively simple to use. Like many things in the world of computers there are new programs coming all the time. You'll have to do a bit of research to find the program most suited to your needs and computer type.

THE FUN STUFF

In the beginning we set out to create a fabric by choosing bead color and texture, and we shaped the fabric by using various techniques. Now we can examine some further methods of creating different effects. Compare beading on the loom to playing the guitar. You can play a few basic chords or you can be another Segovia or Jimmy Hendrix.

Fringe

Fringe can be the finishing touch that makes a piece really work. There are so many forms of fringe that it can take on almost infinite variations. Many of the works in the Gallery section on pages 71–105 illustrate the variety and impact of fringe.

Straight

Straight fringe is the simplest form and uses the warp threads. Center one strand of fringe under every bead in the bottom of the piece or perhaps under every other bead, depending on the effect desired or the materials used. If you are using a larger accent bead or picot at the end of the fringe, you may want to skip every other space or perhaps vary the lengths in a pattern in order to avoid a bunched up, overcrowded look.

You have two warp threads to use for each fringe at the outside edges of the bottom of a piece. You may use one warp thread for the fringe and simply sew the unused one into the work. The better way is to use both warp threads in the fringe which

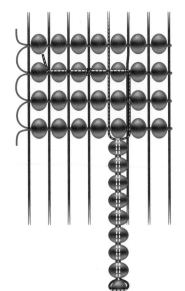

Once you've added a strand of straight fringe, sew the fringe (warp) threads back into the work.

will double the strength of the fringe. The third alternative is to take the extra warp thread down into the fringe as far as possible, then bring it out of the fringe and trim flush.

Knotting fringe threads at the end of the fringe will make the fringe very weak and should be avoided. Instead the fringe (warp) thread should go back up through the fringe and be sewn into the work as shown in the illustration at left.

Kinky Fringe

This describes the fringe not the fringe maker. Kinky fringe can be at the outside edges of the work using the warp threads or it can be applied to the surface of the work

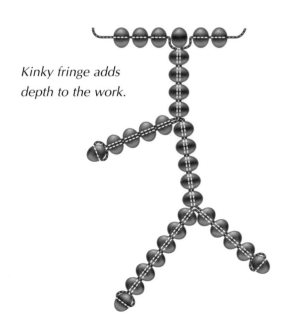

Kinky fringe adds depth to the work.

using a fresh thread introduced into the work. It is a useful tool for adding depth as in Hairy Chest shown on page 54. The figure at lower left shows the thread path used in creating kinky fringe. Kinky fringe can have bugle beads or other accent beads in some or all the legs.

Twisted Fringe

This type of fringe can give a piece an antique look and it adds great texture. To form, put enough beads on the warp thread to get the required length, add one or more marker beads which will guide you in the last step and which will be the tip end of the fringe, then add enough beads to match the length of the first section. Slide the needle down until the eye is about ½ inch from the last bead then roll the needle between the thumb and forefinger to put twist into the thread. It will take about 100 rotations depending on the length of the fringe. Be consistent in the amount of twist in each fringe. Take care that the loose end of the fringe thread does not tangle. Grasp the point where the thread exits the last bead so you do not lose the twist. Pull the needle back up the thread a few inches, and while holding the twist in, insert the needle back into

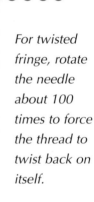

For twisted fringe, rotate the needle about 100 times to force the thread to twist back on itself.

53

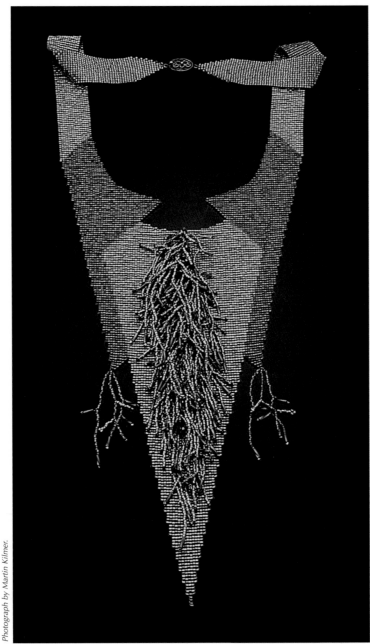

Hairy Chest—Gold. 6" × 8".

the work and pull the end of the fringe up to the work. Grasp the marker bead or beads at the center of the strand. Release the fringe and it should twist up on itself. If the marker beads are not perfectly centered you can untwist the fringe and, while holding the marker beads, let the fringe re-twist. Sew in the fringe thread in the normal way.

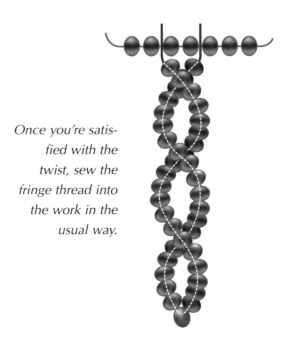

Once you're satisfied with the twist, sew the fringe thread into the work in the usual way.

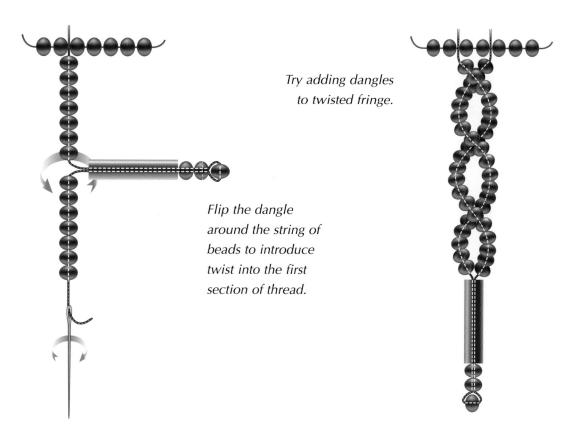

Try adding dangles to twisted fringe.

Flip the dangle around the string of beads to introduce twist into the first section of thread.

You may add dangles at the end of twisted fringe by threading them on as shown in the figures above. It will be necessary to flip the dangle portion around the string of beads about half as many times as the thread is twisted in order to introduce twist in the first section of thread.

Vertical Fringe

I call this Hedgehog fringe because of the tactile quality of the finished work. It adds a third dimension to the piece. Each stack of beads forming the fringe is held directly on top of the base bead. The figure at the top of page 56 shows the thread path. Varying the height of the stacks of beads can give a sculpted look. This is a very simple fringe but can be difficult and tedious if the whole piece is covered.

The beads in the base need to have large holes because there will be many threads passed through each of them. I recommend using Delicas for the base. The type and size of the beads in the fringe will affect the tex-

55

56 *Fire and Ice. 5½" × 13" × 1".*

ture of the finished work. A looser texture can also be achieved by skipping some of the base beads.

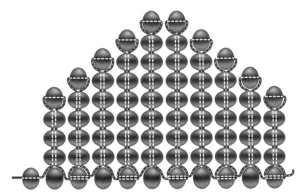

For vertical fringe, each stack of beads is held directly on top of a base bead.

Curly Fringe

This fringe is easy to make and gives an effect similar to kinky fringe. Take the return thread back into the work and pull tight to

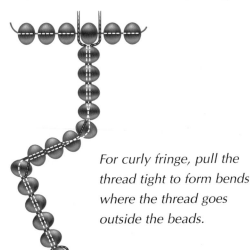

For curly fringe, pull the thread tight to form bends where the thread goes outside the beads.

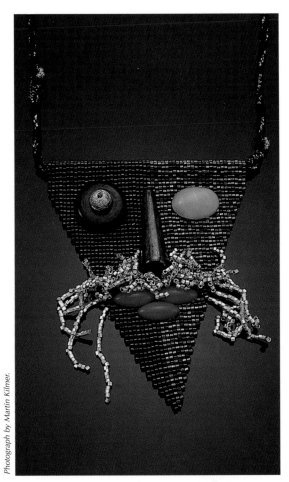

Fu Manchu on a Bad Hair Day. 3" × 4".

woven, or it can be added after the piece is woven, either on loom or off loom. One thing different about edge fringe is that the beads are orientated in the same direction as the beads in the body of the piece. The figure below shows the thread path for adding fringe to either side while the weaving is being done. Edge fringe can be added after the weaving is complete by introducing a new thread and adding the fringe in the same manner that end fringe is added.

Edge fringe may be added to either side as the piece is being woven.

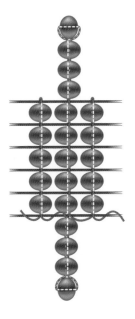

create the bends where the thread goes outside the beads. The tightness of the bends is determined by how hard you pull.

Edge Fringe

Fringe coming out of the edge of the weaving can be done while the piece is being

Dangles

Dangles are fringe with muscle. A series of large accent beads or a large bunch of small beads can be used independently or in conjunction with regular fringe of some sort. Dangles are usually attached at corners

57

and points as in Southwest Construction shown at left to provide an accent. Dangles work best in odd numbers.

Negative Space

You may want to leave an opening in the woven work to display a feature bead or leave vacant to add emphasis to your design. Most of the problems involved in doing this deal with the need to sew in the exposed warp threads that result when the opening is created. There are three methods to accomplish this effect. Often more than one method will be used in the same piece.

Interrupted and Supplemental Warp

When you come to a point in the weaving where you want to leave an opening,

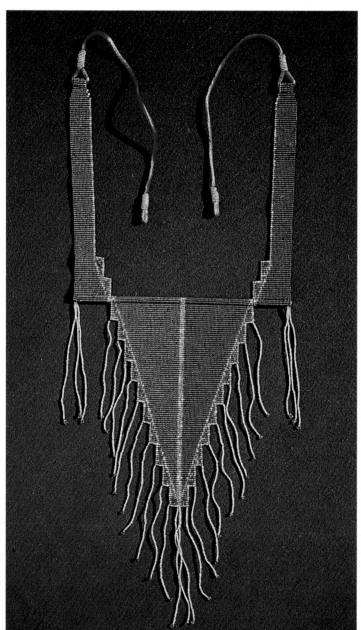

Photograph by Jim Thornton.

58   *Southwest Construction. 6" × 15".*

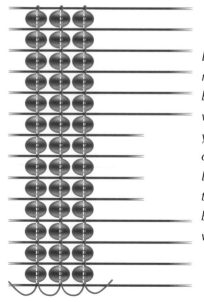

Leave a negative space by cutting the warp where you want the opening. Leave enough thread to sew back in to the weaving.

Photograph by Martin Kilmer.

School of Fishes. 8" × 21". This neckpiece uses both interrupted/supplemental warp and the pull and pray methods to create negative spaces.

59

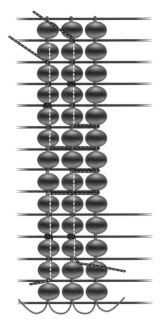

Sew the cut warp threads back into the work.

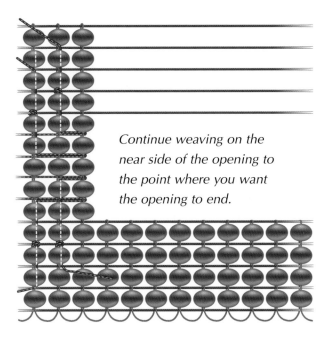

Continue weaving on the near side of the opening to the point where you want the opening to end.

Introduce new warp threads to replace those you cut.

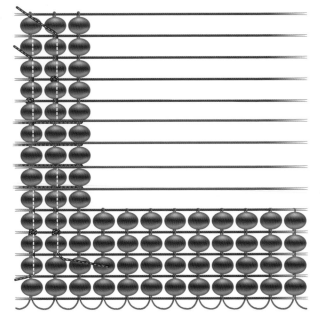

one of the methods you can use involves interrupting, or cutting the warp where you want the opening. You will cut the warps far enough from the weaving to leave a thread long enough to sew back into the weaving. When you cut a warp thread, tie off the loose end that's away from the work at the end of the loom to prevent some other warp thread from sagging or coming loose. You should also sew in the cut warp at this point. Then proceed to weave the material on the near side of the opening up to the place where you want to end the opening. At this point you will add supplemental warp over the top of the weaving to replace the warps previously cut. You can then continue weaving across the entire width as

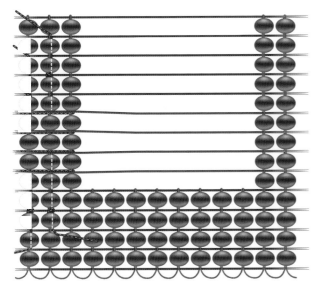

Continue weaving across the entire width as before the opening.

before the opening. There will be a section on the away side of the hole that is not woven. This weaving can be completed at any time. I usually wait until all the weaving on the near side is completed then turn the loom around and finish up any unfinished areas of the opposite side.

Pull and Pray

Another method of leaving an opening involves leaving the warp threads in place but simply not using them. When the piece is finished and cut off the loom you will pull the warp threads through the piece creating a loop that can be cut in half leaving two threads long enough to be sewn back into the weaving.

There are several things that can cause you grief in doing the Pull and Pray. If you have speared any of the warp threads while weaving, then the warp will not pull through. If you know that you will want to use this method, you should check each row for speared warp threads while weaving.

If you didn't leave enough warp thread at the end of the piece you will not have comfortably long threads to sew back into the weaving. This is where a short sharps needle comes in handy.

If your opening is very far from the ends of the piece, you will not be able to pull the warp threads through the weaving. This is where the interrupted, supplemental warp method would work better.

Distorted Warp

A third method of creating a small open area is to simply pull the warp threads aside

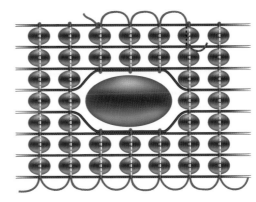

Create a negative space by pulling the warp thread aside as you weave.

to leave an opening. This can be used for incorporating a larger bead into the fabric. This is not as neat as using the interrupted, supplemental warp method, because it leaves exposed warp threads at the sides of the opening. Holes involving more than two warp threads should be done with the interrupted, supplemental method.

Mixing Bead Sizes and Types

It is possible to mix bead sizes within a piece in a number of ways. Keep in mind that you want the work to be even, without large irregularities in shape.

One way is to mix bead sizes in alternate rows. Warp the loom for the widest beads, then choose combinations of smaller beads

Mixing beads of different sizes creates an interesting texture.

that equal the width of a large bead. This can create an interesting textural effect.

Mixing slightly larger beads into a weaving is not a problem if they are incorporated on the diagonal or in a random manner where the extra height or width of the larger beads averages out within the height or width of the weaving. It may be necessary to use some narrower beads around the large one to keep the edges of the work even.

If the larger beads are placed in a vertical stack there will be a vertical deformity in the work that is usually undesirable.

Bugle beads or other taller beads can be incorporated into the weaving by interrupting warps then weaving in the larger beads on the weft threads. (See Art Deco 1 on page 41.) Wider beads can be incorporated by using multiple rows of weaving for each bead.

Beads On the Warp

If every warp thread will have beads strung on it, the easiest method is to string a quantity of beads on the warp thread before starting to warp the loom. I do this by putting the spool of warp thread on the floor and stringing on about ten feet of beads. This is about as much as can be done without getting tangled up. I then feed on as many as are necessary for each warp as the loom is being warped. If there are many beads on each warp thread, you will probably have to warp in stages of a few warps at a time.

When all the warps are in place, push the beads to the end of the warp threads in the direction you will be weaving. You can then slide them down on the warps and incorporate them into the weaving as needed.

If the beads going on the warps are bigger in diameter than the width of the beads being woven into the body of the piece, or if a more open effect is wanted, you may use two warp threads for each pre-strung row of beads.

To use two warp threads for each pre-strung row of beads, put two warp threads on the needle while stringing the beads on, then separate the warp threads in the springs while warping the loom.

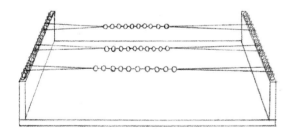

You may use two warp threads for each pre-strung row of beads and separate the warps in the springs.

Blending and Shading

It is possible to create a new color or to blend from one color to another by simply mixing two or more colors together in varying combinations.

If you just want to create a new color you will blend two or more other colors until you have the desired result, then as you use the mix you'll pick up the beads randomly. Be sure to mix enough for the work at hand, because unless you carefully measured amounts of each color used you won't be able to exactly duplicate the first mix. This technique works best if the color changes are subtle. By matching similar values (the lightness or darkness of a color) you can be assured that the colors will blend well. See the Gallery section for examples.

If you want to start with one color and progress to another, you may want to set up a formula for adding set amounts of color through the progression from color A to color B. For instance, if you want to start with blue, then go to purple and then to black, and do it in forty rows of weaving, your formula might look like this:

All Blue
Next five rows: Add 1/4 purple
Next five rows: Add another 1/4 purple
Next five rows: Add another 1/4 purple
Next five rows: Add another 1/4 purple
All purple
Next five rows: Add 1/4 black
Next five rows: Add another 1/4 black
Next five rows: Add another 1/4 black
Next five rows: Add another 1/4 black
All black
Another option is to just go for it.

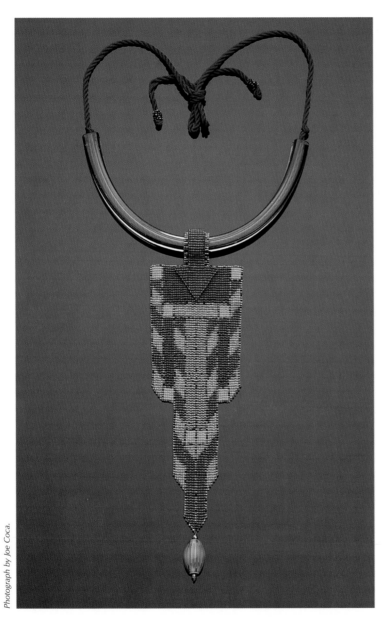

No Martini for Frank. 6" × 12". Curved bead by Olive Glass, chevron by Heron Glass, finished with silk cord. Folded and layered at top for structural strength

64

If you are doing a necklace with straps using this type of graduated blending, you will want to work the straps on both sides before changing the blend to the next step.

Folding and Layering

Loomwork folds nicely in the horizontal plane. It does not fold in the vertical plane or diagonally.

Folding can be very useful for adding strength to the loomwork, and in creating an added dimension.

Generally when I fold beadwork back over itself, I glue it together then sew it down as well. When three or more layers are glued and sewn together the work becomes as stiff as plywood. To glue, use E-6000 adhesive, which is quite thick, or similar adhesive. Spread it evenly and fairly thickly on both surfaces to be adhered. Let it get tacky before pressing the beadwork together so that the adhesive does not squeeze through the beads or out the edges of the work. Once pressed together let it dry thoroughly before handling. Sew the edges of the folded portion down.

Embellishment

Adding surface embellishment in the form of beads or other decorative detail is an excellent way to enhance a woven base. This kind of embellishment can become the focus of the piece or may just enhance the design.

For the most part, surface embellishment will be sewn on but glue can be used if there is no other option. In the case of the necklace shown at right, the large abalone disk is glued on using E-6000 adhesive.

Bars, Tubes, and Rods

Insufficient structural strength can sometimes be remedied by hanging the woven work from a support. This is an excellent method of supporting the weight of a large bead, or for supporting a woven structure with no inherent strength of its own. Pages 48 through 51 show several ways this technique can be used.

When enclosing a bar or tube for support, I sew the woven material together around the bar or tube using the stitch outlined below.

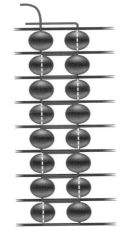

When enclosing a bar for support, sew the woven material back together following this thread path.

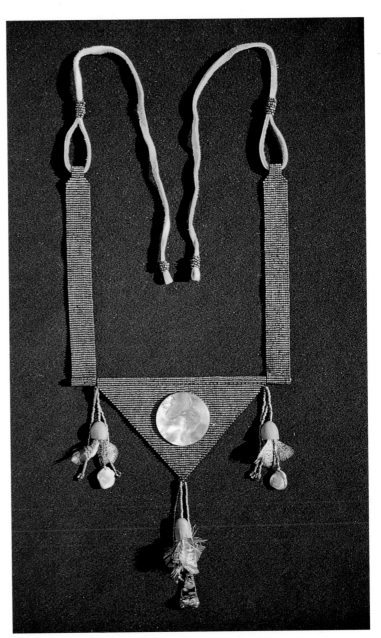

Abalone Disk. 6 " × 10" plus ties.

In pieces such as those shown on pages 48 and 65, the straps are woven separately from the pendant. After they are sewn around the support rod they must be sewn together and the opening at the end of the rod must be closed with a bead to keep the rod from coming out.

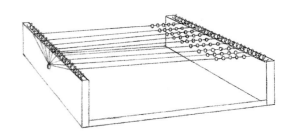

Open Weave

Creating open weave on the loom is quite simple and adaptable for a variety of projects. Before you start to set up the loom

To create an open weave, determine the size of the openings and pre-string the warps with the appropriate number of beads. Then warp the loom leaving the appropriate amount of space between each warp thread.

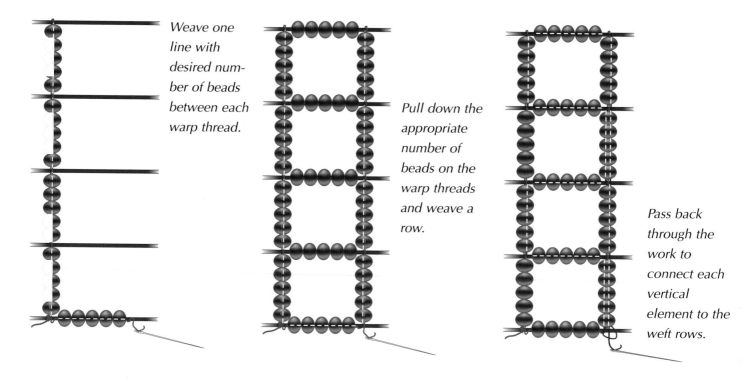

Weave one line with desired number of beads between each warp thread.

Pull down the appropriate number of beads on the warp threads and weave a row.

Pass back through the work to connect each vertical element to the weft rows.

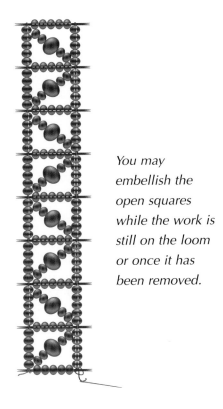

You may embellish the open squares while the work is still on the loom or once it has been removed.

beads on each line in case you change your mind or miscount.

Warp the loom leaving a space between each warp thread equal to the width of the square, in this case 5 beads. Each warp will have 110+ beads on it. When the warping is completed, slide all the beads to the end of the loom that you will be working toward. Weave one line putting 5 beads between each warp thread.

Pull down 5 beads on each warp thread. Pass the needle up through the 5 beads on the near outside warp thread and weave a row across. When the second row is complete you will go back through the work to connect each vertical element to the weft rows.

Continue in this manner until the weaving is completed. Now the piece can be cut from the loom and all the loose warp and weft threads can be sewn in by knotting at the junctions and sewing in the thread ends in the regular way.

Embellishments in the form of beads can be added within each square while the piece is on the loom or after it has been finished.

OTHER METHODS OF INTEREST

Here are some interesting variations of beading on a loom. These are not methods that I use, but ones I find interesting and I present them for your consideration.

you must determine the size of the project and the size of the openings in the project.

For example, I am doing a rectangle that is 5½" long and 2" wide and has ¼" openings. I am using Delica beads. This means I will have a piece 22 squares long and 8 squares wide, each with 5 beads to the side. All of the beads forming the vertical portions of the squares will be strung on the warp thread before the loom is warped. Thus I will string 9 verticals of 5 beads times 22 squares or 110 beads per line for a total of 990 beads. I recommend putting extra

67

Four Selvedge Loomwork

This technique is based on ancient Peruvian and Navajo weaving techniques, and was originally conceived by Phylis Morrison of Cambridge, Massachusetts. Theresa Guthrie, a student of Phylis's has developed the method that she calls the "No Warps!" technique. With this technique you avoid the step of weaving in all those loose warp ends.

A loom can be constructed of almost any sturdy four-sided object, such as a picture frame. Combine this with a few sticks, cardboard, lacing, needles, thread, and beads and you are ready to go.

The "No Warps!" technique is useful for weaving small projects such as bracelets, trims, and pendants. With experience you might do large projects such as tapestries. The actual weaving on this type of loom is done using basic weaving techniques and methods. Theresa offers workshops on her method and continues to develop the technique.

Two-Needle Weaving

Jules Kliot of Lacis in Berkeley has shown me a method of weaving using two needles. This method can be used when weaving on a large tapestry loom. The idea is to use a long needle under the warps to pick up the beads, and then once the beads are pushed up into place and checked for color a shorter needle is brought through the beads on top of the warp threads. Thus there are two weft threads, one above and one below the warp. With this method the beader can pick up beads of each color on the bottom needle without counting. After bringing the top needle through the proper amount of that color, any extra beads on

Photograph by Joe Coca.

For Theresa Guthrie's "No Warps!" technique, construct a loom of a sturdy four-sided object.

the bottom needle can be dropped and the next color added.

Beads as Warp and Weft

Kathy Dannerbeck and Donna Kaplan have developed a method of bead weaving on traditional fabric looms using beads on the warp or the weft or both. Their aim is to create fabrics that incorporate beads within the fabric rather than adding them later as embellishment. They also feel that this type of weaving is faster and produces stronger results than basic bead weaving. They have created purses and necklaces as well as fabric for garments or other uses.

Heddle Loom

The use of the heddle for bead weaving was probably introduced into the Great Lakes region by French traders or missionaries in the mid to late 1800s. Heddle weaving with beads developed with the availability of seed beads and thread. Most of the samples of heddle weaving from the 1800s are by Native Americans from the Woodland Tribes.

The principle of the heddle bead loom is exactly the same as basic fabric looms. The heddle is used to create a "shed," or opening between sets of warp threads, which allow the bead weft to be passed through. When the shed is reversed the bead weft is locked into place. Each row of beading has only one weft thread.

Kathy Dannerbeck and Donna Kaplan use beads as warp and weft on traditional fabric looms.

69

Much traditional Native American beadwork was done on a heddle loom.

John Lotter, now deceased, has been the person most responsible for preserving and promoting the traditional Native American uses of the heddle loom. He taught in the Chicago area and manufactured and sold looms and heddles. His detailed plans for both loom and heddle were published in *Whispering Wind* magazine in the winter 1992 issue. His loom design looks like a simplistic fabric loom.

John Lotter at his loom. Photographs courtesy of Whispering Wind *magazine.*

GALLERY OF CONTEMPORARY LOOMWORK

The following pages exemplify a great diversity of loomed beadwork styles. Limited in scope by space constraints and personal knowledge, this body of work nonetheless demonstrates the many wonderful variations of one simple technique. I have included work at both ends of the scale in terms of size and degree of difficulty to demonstrate the possibilities of beading on the loom and to inspire creativity.

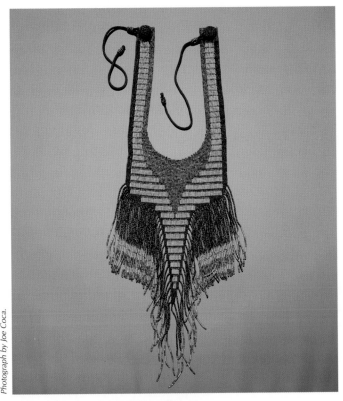

Photograph by Joe Coca.

Don Pierce. Coos Bay, Oregon.
Shimmy & Shake. *16"W × 18"H plus ties.*

Why does man create?

Is it mans purpose on earth to express himself, to bring form to thought and to discover meaning in experience?

Or is it just something to do when he's bored?

—Calvin, *Calvin and Hobbes*
by Bill Watterson, 1995

71

Photograph by Joe Coca.

Margie Deeb. Roswell, Georgia.

The Mantle of the Weaver Woman. *7"W × 44"L. A mantle-scarf embellished with semi-precious gemstones, bronze and glass beads. Hundreds of unique fringe elements.*

Photograph by Neil Moore.

Tidal Pool Treasure. *8"W × 32"H. Includes semi-precious gemstones, shell, wood, and glass seed and bugle beads. Used the gather and pull (deformed warp) technique to form openings for large beads.*

73

Photograph by Laura Willits.

Laura Willits. Seattle, Washington.
Reservoir. 10¾"W × 13¼"H. Size 11° seed beads. Computer-generated graph from a watercolor monoprint. Collection of the artist.

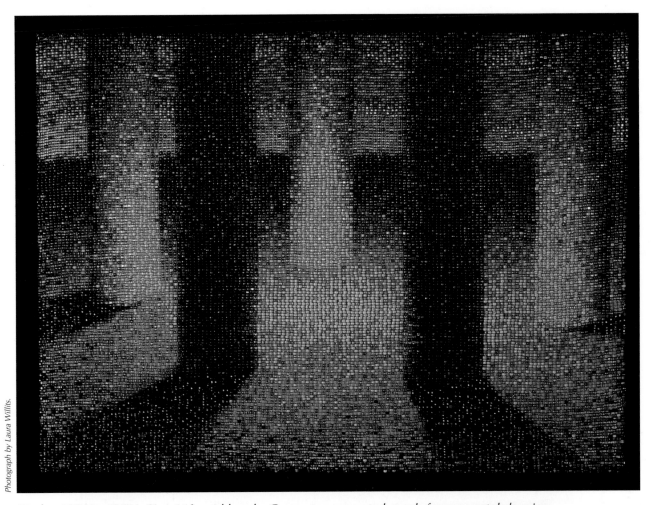

Photograph by Laura Willits.

Circle. *13"W × 9⅜"H. Size 11° seed beads. Computer-generated graph from a pastel drawing. Private collection.*

Photograph by Joe Coca.

Delinda V. Amura. Los Angeles, California.
Vision Through Space, amulet necklace. 1½"W × 4"H plus straps. Lattice weaving with beads on the warp. Side gussets added to form a dimensional bag. Accented with turquoise, amethyst, aventurine, brass, turquoise donuts, and brass bumblebees. Finished with a lattice neck chain and twisted fringe.

Photograph by Joe Coca.

Kathie Schroeder. Tucson, Arizona.
Grass in the Wind. *1½"W × 7½"H. Loom worked with surface "fringe."*

Photograph by Joe Coca.

Frieda Bates. Artesia, New Mexico.

Flame. *5"W × 20"H woven with size 13° cut seed beads. Fringe of antique needle bugle beads with 4mm smooth round roundels and 4mm faceted round Czech fire polish beads.*

Photograph by Joe Coca.

Patience. *4½"W × 20"H. Size 13° seed beads. Fringe contains 2mm and 4mm Austrian crystals, 4mm smooth round and 4mm roundels.*

Photograph by Joe Coca.

Photograph by Joe Coca.

Photograph by Joe Coca.

Theresa Guthrie. Concord, Massachusetts.
Girl Before The Mirror—A Second Look.
(Above left.) 5"W × 7"H. Based on a Picasso painting. Delica beads woven with the "No Warps!" Technique (see page 68).

Fuzzy Wuzzy Boogie. *(Left.) Cuff is 2"W × 6"L stitched to metal bracelet with Ultrasuede backing. Black keys in vertical fringe with music charms. Woven with the "No Warps!" Technique.*

Crazy Quilt. *(Above.) Cuff is 1½"W × 6"L stitched to metal bracelet with Ultrasuede backing. Woven with the "No Warps!" Technique.*

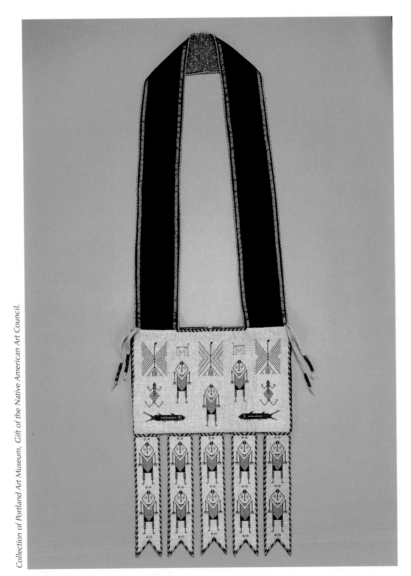

Daryel Lopez. Gresham, Oregon.
Bandolier Bag. *14"W × 19½"H plus shoulder strap. Seed beads and fabric. Tells the story of how coyote gave man a mouth so he could eat sturgeon.*

81

Photograph by Joe Coca.

Judith Durant. Loveland, Colorado.
Miniature Carpet. *9½"W × 17"H. 32,340 size 11° seed beads.*

Photograph by Earl Olsen.

Donna Kaplan. North Bend, Washington.

Future Anachronisms. Beaded Logging Boots. *Woven fabric panels with beads as weft in 8 and 16 shaft figurative overshot weave structure are velcroed to the boots. Beads size 24° to 11°. This pair of boots attempts to tell a story about the Snoqualmie Valley and what is happening to the land as an old way of life fades and a new one takes over. The original boots had been discarded and slung over the fence at a logging yard.*

83

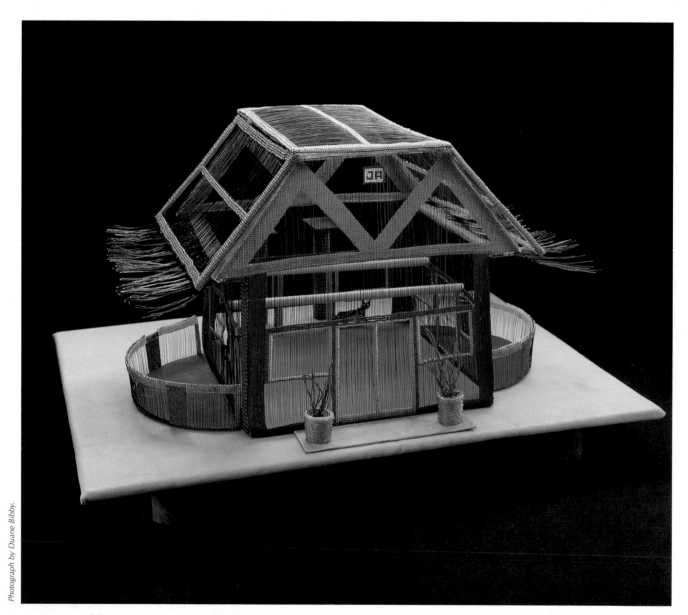

Photograph by Duane Bibby.

Jeanette Ahlgren. Fortuna, California.
Bird House, *a.k.a.* House of Cats. *14"H × 24"W × 18"D. Annealed steel wire warp and polyester weft. Size 11° seed beads.*

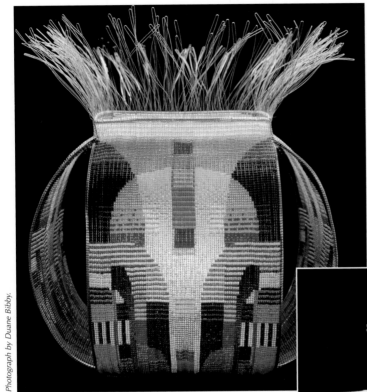

Monterey. *10"W × 12"H × 10"D. Size 11° seed beads. Brass wire warp with polyester weft.*

Sabotage (Green orchid).
11"W × 11"H × 11"D. Size 11° seed beads woven on stainless steel wire warps with polyester weft.

Photograph by Mike Camacho.

Denise Kavanagh. St. Charles, Illinois.
Spirit of Kaffe *waist belt. 5"W × 5"H with Kumihimo tie.*

Photograph by Kathy Dannerbeck.

Kathy Dannerbeck. Bellevue, Washington.

Woven Drawstring Bag. *7"W × 5"H. Woven on a four-harness jack loom using an overshot grouped-warp thread pattern. The beads were woven in as weft in overshot.*

Photograph by Larry Brown.

Larry Brown. Brooklyn, New York.
Beaded Kente Shawl. *4"W × 40"L. Size 10° seed beads, Mali mud cloth, and Cowrie shells. Influence of the Maasai and Nbebele peoples of Africa and Cherokee Native Americans show in the bold colors and geometric designs.*

Photograph by Larry Brown.

Beaded Kente Shawl. *4"W × 40"L.*
Size 10° seed beads, Mali mud cloth,
leather, Cowrie shells.

Neck appointment. *6½"W × 12"H.*
Size 10° seed beads, Cowrie shells.

Photograph by Larry Brown.

89

Photograph by Joe Coca.

Doug Johnson. Newburyport, Massachusetts.
Boston Skyline. *43"W × 22½"H. 190,800 size 11°*
seed beads. From his original photo taken from
East Boston. Woven in one piece.

Cathedral Night. *An interpretation of purgatory. 33½"W × 24"H. 164,000 size 11° seed beads. Woven in one piece.*

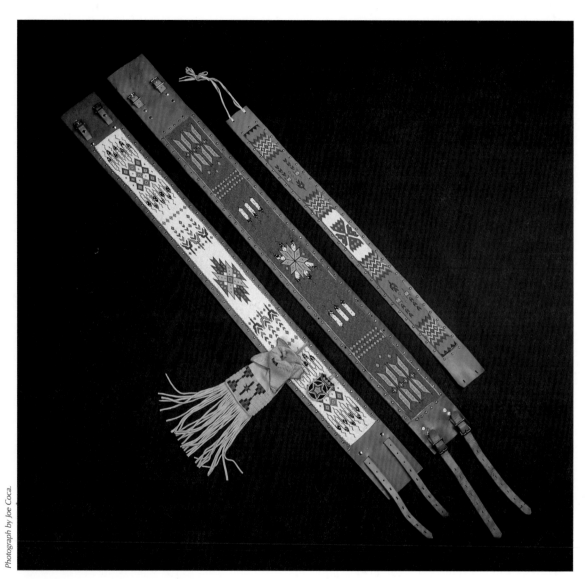

Photograph by Joe Coca.

David Dean. Galesburg, Illinois.

Straight Dance Belts. All three are part of personal dance regalia.

White belt. 3¼"W × 36"L. Size 13° Czech seed beads with medicine pouch.

Red belt. 3½"W × 37"L. Size 4-o (equivalent to size 12°) antique Italian Cheyenne white lined beads.

Blue belt. 1⅞"W × 30"L size 13° Czech seed beads. Child's belt.

Photograph by Joe Coca.

Hat band. *½"W × 23"L. Size 13° Czech cuts.*

Otter drop decoration. *Part of dance regalia. 2½"W × 18"L.*

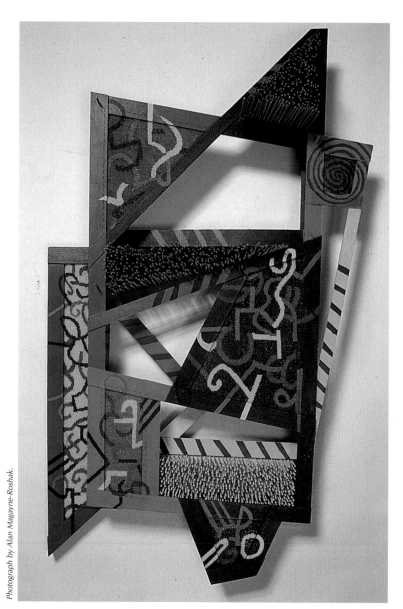

Photograph by Alan Magayne-Roshak.

Peggy Kendellen. Portland, Oregon.
Chimerical. *Wall piece is 23"W × 39"H × 6"D. Size 11° seed beads, wood. Collection of Nieman Marcus.*

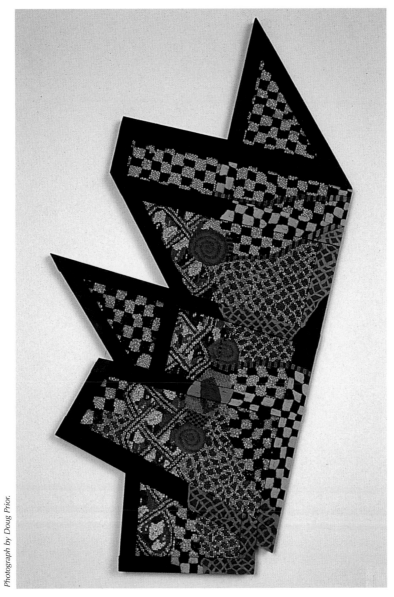

Photograph by Doug Prior.

Three Red Spirals. *Wall piece is 15"W × 30½"H × 1"D.*
Size 11° seed beads, wood. Collection of Northwestern Mutual
Life Insurance.

Photograph by Joe Coca.

Ann Shafer. Los Alamos, New Mexico.

Anasazi Snake. *5"W × 13"H. Loomworked with irregular boundaries and asymmetrical design. Size 11° beads.*

Photograph by Joe Coca.

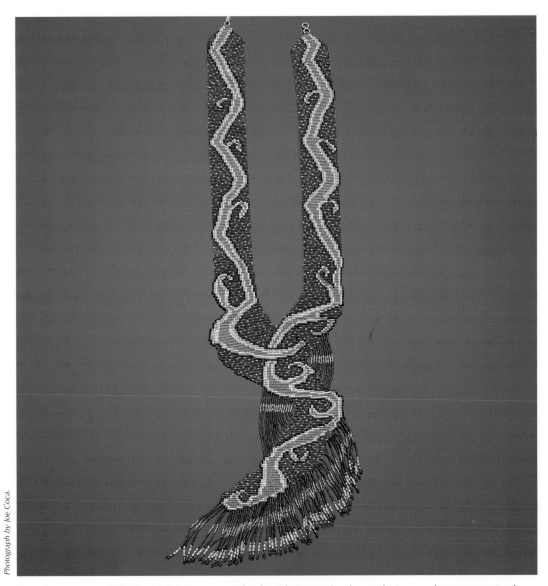

Entwinement. 4½"W × 19"H. Loomworked with irregular boundaries and asymmetrical design. Incorporates beaded warps. Size 15° beads.

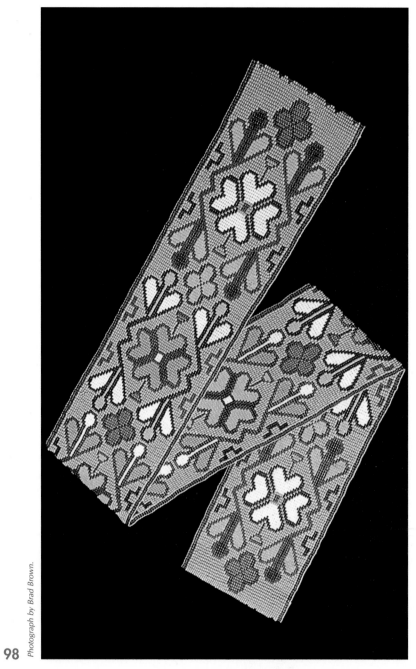

Photograph by Brad Brown.

98

Adam Lovell. Edmond, Oklahoma.

Photograph by Brad Brown.

The artist posed in fancy dance regalia of his own design.

Dance belt. *3½"W × 36"H. Size 11° seed beads. Collection of Ty Stewart.*

Carol Perrenoud. Wilsonville, Oregon.
Chantecler of Cockaigne. *3"W × 18"H.
Size 20° antique beads. 800 beads
per square inch. Peyote stitched corn
and shaded twisted fringe.*

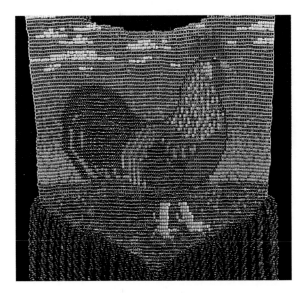

Photograph by Carol Perrenoud.

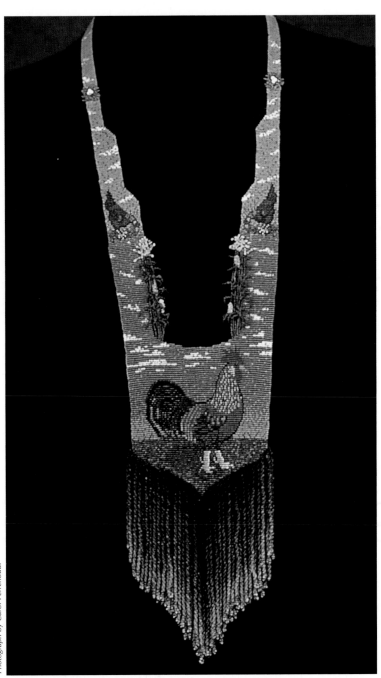

Photographs by Masayuki Tsuksui.

Takako Sako. Tokyo, Japan.

The World of Genji. *Dolls wearing traditional dresses of Japanese Heian era. Japanese traditional kimono is tailored into a flat sheet. The traditional dress of female doll is called Jyunihitoe and comprises 12 kimonos. Each doll is about 6" high.*

Hataori Bijin—Weaving Beauty. *23½"W × 28¾"H. From a 1765 multicolored woodprint by Harunobu. 26 colors of Delica beads, 170,000 beads.*

Photographs by Masayuki Tsuksui.

Fuhjin and Raisin—The God of Wind and the God of Thunder. *Each about 20"W × 26"H. From an ancient screen painting by Soutatsu. Shows the humor and tenderness of the Gods. Fuhjin is 130,000 beads, Raisin is 140,000 beads.*

101

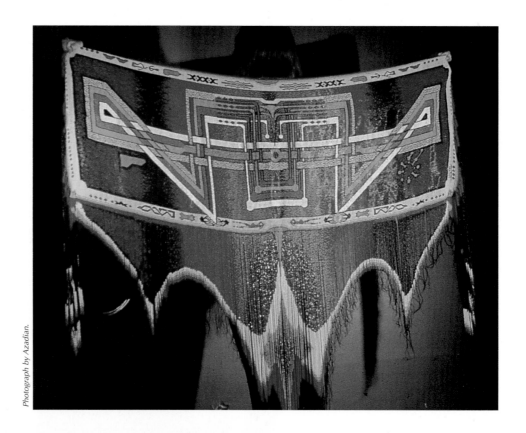

Photograph by Azadian.

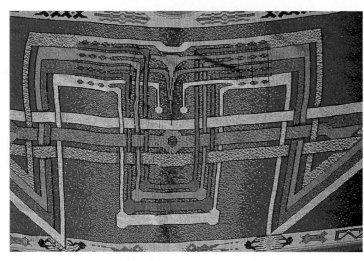

Talbot. Austin, Texas.
Beaded Shawl. *Loomed and fringed seed beads,
unbacked. 9'W × 5'L with fringe fully extended.
Approximately 750,000 beads.*

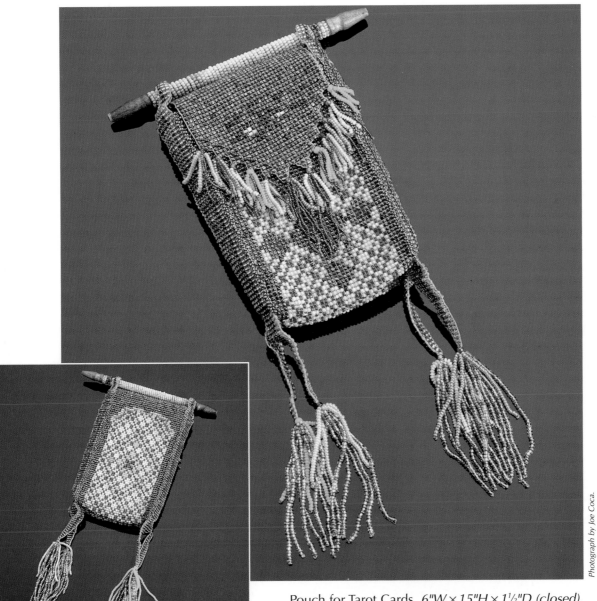

Photograph by Joe Coca.

Pouch for Tarot Cards. *6"W × 15"H × 1½"D (closed).*
Seed beads with silk liner and wood.

Photograph by Gary L Betts.

Virginia Blakelock. Wilsonville, Oregon.
Daphnis Nerii-Oleander Hawk Moth. *9"W × 16"H. Combines loomwork with the techniques of Egyptian broad collars. Size 16° antique seed beads, 494 beads per square inch.*

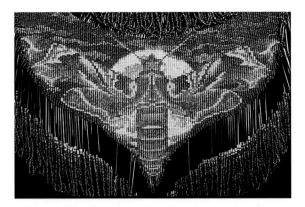

Detail of Daphnis.

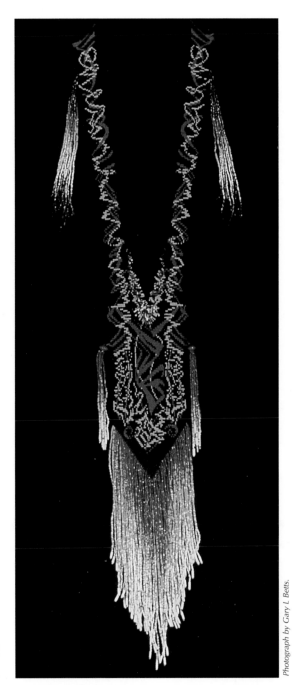

Firecracker. *3"W × 30"H. Size 15° antique seed beads, 368 beads per square inch.*

Photograph by Gary L Betts.

Photograph by Gary L Betts.

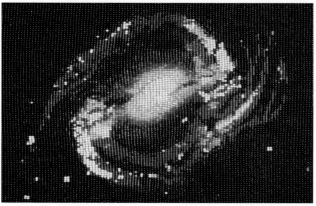

Galaxy NGC1300. *Loomworked collar, 12¼"W×12¾"H. Size 18° antique seed beads, 609 beads per square inch. 1238 warp threads are finished off in short fringe.*

Japanese Seed Beads, Size 15°

Selected Bibliography

Amura, Delinda Vannebrightyn. *The Illuminated Beading Manuscripts, Book 2 The Loom.* South Pasadena, California: Fairy Wing Press, 1997.

Blakelock, Virginia L. *Those Bad Bad Beads.* Wilsonville, Oregon: Virginia Blakelock, 1988.

Dannerbeck, Kathryn & Donna Kaplan. *Beads as Warp and Weft.* Bellevue, Washington: Beads and Beyond, 1998.

Dubin, Lois Sherr. *The History of Beads.* New York: Harry N. Abrams, Inc., 1987.

Durant, Judith & Jean Campbell. *The Beader's Companion.* Loveland, Colorado: Interweave Press, 1998.

Kliot, Jules and Kaethe. *Bead Work, Second Edition.* Berkeley, California: Lacis Publications, 1996.

Lotter, John. "Heddle Loom Beadwork." *Whispering Winds Magazine* Volume 25, Number 6, Winter 1992.

Moss, Kathlyn & Alice Scherer. *The New Beadwork.* New York: Harry N. Abrams, Inc., 1992.

Presslar, Pam. *A Beadworker's Took-Book.* Tucson, Arizona: Polar Publishing Company, 1995.

Sako, Takako. *Beadweaving Accessories.* Berkeley, California: Lacis Publications, 1998.

INDEX